D0514179

9030 00002 1673 4

Charles Dickens
on
travel

edited by Pete Orford

ET REMOTISSIMA PROPE

'on'

'on'

Published by Hesperus Press Limited
4 Rickett Street, London sw6 1ru
www.hesperuspress.com

First published 1836–63
This collection first published by Hesperus Press Limited, 2009

Introduction and notes © Pete Orford, 2009

Designed and typeset by Fraser Muggeridge studio
Printed in Jordan by Jordan National Press

isbn: 978-1-84391-612-3

Contents

Introduction

As a writer Dickens wanted his efforts to not only entertain his readers, but educate and benefit them as well. In the preface to *The Pickwick Papers* he concludes that 'if any of his imperfect descriptions, while they afford amusements in the perusal, should induce only one reader to think better of his fellow men, and to look upon the brighter and more kindly side of human nature, he would indeed be proud and happy to have led to such a result.' The champion of the masses, Dickens' novels and articles encouraged the reader to journey alongside the narrator and characters, broadening their own horizons as they did so, and this last aspect was an idea taken up literally in Dickens' own travels and subsequent accounts of such adventures. His talent of observation, of both people and places, lends an immediate advantage to his travel writing as he reports on the sights and sounds around him.

This is evident in Dickens' earliest writing, *Sketches by Boz*, from which is taken the first article collected here, 'The Last Cab Driver and the First Omnibus Cad' (1836). As a young man his experience was still limited to his home country, but the sketches are an encouragement to look again at the sights around us and see the stories that are otherwise taken for granted. After all, the everyday and exotic are defined by where we originate from, and just as the Tower of Pisa might prove otherworldly to an Englishman, so the Hackney cabs of London can be just as worthy of attention to those unfamiliar with them. Dickens faithfully conveys the experience of transport in the nineteenth-century metropolis with trademark humour and admiration for the rogues he identifies, fleshing out the past with the sordid reality of the characters who inhabited it, and the legacy of the piece is that, whilst redefining the everyday for his contemporaries, to the modern reader it provides a detailed snapshot of travel in a past age.

Another detailed account of yesterday's transport is provided in the second article 'The Passage Out', taken from *American Notes* (1842), where Dickens gives a very subjective, intimate and truthful account of travelling by steamer. Though Dickens' travels to both America and Italy would result in published works, the reader is left with no doubt that both these journeys were decidedly for pleasure rather than business: *American Notes* and *Pictures from Italy* have a very personal, individual feel about them. After all, Dickens was aware that there were already a number of travel guides available, and did not try to compete with this 'stock of information', as he called it, by producing definitive guides of where to go. Instead he delighted in seeing the places he wanted to see, often going off the beaten track; his visit to America involved tours around prisons and asylums. His writing has as much to say about human nature as it does about the new world he visited, and the pace of the transatlantic journey in 'The Passage Out' is underlined and enhanced by the dynamics of himself, the crew and his fellow passengers.

But occasionally his fellow men did not warm to being part of Dickens' writings. Though dubbed 'Mr Popular Sentimentality' by Trollope, Dickens' observations were also interpreted as caustic or hostile, especially when writing of abroad. But Dickens was simply applying the same skills of observation he used in his own country, and his willingness to poke fun at foreigners merely reflected his same willingness to poke fun at his own countrymen,

> As I have never, in writing fiction, had any disposition to soften what is ridiculous or wrong at home, I hope (and believe) that the good-humoured people of the United States are not generally disposed to quarrel with me for carrying the same usage abroad.

Dickens' naivety of international relations was revealed when the 'good-humoured people' of pre-civil war America *were* disposed to quarrel with Dickens' account of his travels abroad; little wonder given his horror at the slave trade and his mocking of the New World's sense of self-importance. The subsequent furore influenced Dickens to affirm his disinterestedness when writing his next travel fiction, *Pictures from Italy* (1843). He took especial care in the introduction to further distance himself from the authoritative style of other travel guides, making it clear that these were only his own impressions, 'a series of faint reflections – mere shadows in the water', which he invited the reader to share. Though he marvelled at what he perceived as the gaudiness of Roman Catholic rituals, on the whole he abstained from criticism of the country and the result is a work which is very much focused on the narrator's personal experience and interests. The extract here, 'By Verona, Mantua and Milan', shows the author's own preoccupations, with his love of Shakespeare dominating his trip to Verona, his encounter with a cicerone occupying his impressions of Mantua, and his trip to Milan giving way to discussions of art. The narrative style is very conversational, Dickens' triumph as a travel writer being to invite us in as a friend to listen to his holiday tales.

Indeed, the travel writing and non-fiction work which Dickens produced, freed from the necessity to focus on fictional characters and plots, is as close as he got to a published autobiography. Given the way in which Dickens foregrounds himself in these accounts, it is therefore important for the modern reader to remind themselves of exactly who is telling the story. The popular image of Dickens to the modern reader is the fatherly figure with the beard and moustache, yet this is a direct result of the publicity photographs distributed during his second tour of America in 1867–9. For readers of *Sketches by Boz*, *American Notes*, *Pictures from Italy*, and his journals, the enduring image during this time was the 1838 portrait by Daniel Maclise that appeared in *Nicholas Nickleby*, when Dickens was a young man in his late twenties. Though less familiar now than the bearded Dickens, nonetheless the image of the younger Dickens is far more appropriate to his travel writing, as his first voyages to America and Italy were undertaken while he was in his early thirties: we are therefore dealing with the writings of a young man out to see the world, with all the enthusiasm and naivety we might expect of such a traveller.

It is interesting therefore to compare the two articles *A Flight* (1851) and *The Calais Night Mail* (1863), which recount the same journey to France but as told by two different people; the first experienced by Charles Dickens, thirty-nine year old author of comic fiction who had just completed his middle novel, *David Copperfield*, and the second written by Charles Dickens, fifty-one year old literary celebrity, engaged on reading tours across the United Kingdom. Consequently, while each journey is similar, both referring to the train across, the ferry, the customs office, and those first moments in France, the two accounts contrast in tone. The first author is both excited and excitable, wondering at the marvel of modern transport and the speed with which he can travel to Paris, while the second author regards his earlier self as 'a maundering young wretch' and now travels with both familiarity and weariness; he is inherently tired of travelling, beginning his journey with a wish to stay put in the comfortable surroundings of Dover, then ending with a sense of relief to be in the comfortable surroundings of Paris.

Beyond the immediate publication of his travels in non-fiction, Dickens' experiences abroad also provided fuel for his novels. Dickens consistently used first-hand knowledge of locations in which the adventures took place, hence so many of his novels occurring within London and the surrounding area. Consequently, whenever his characters go abroad, their journeys are limited to those places within Dickens's own experience. The advantage is an intimate knowledge of setting and scene that Dickens used to complement his adventures and comment upon the emotional journeys of the characters. In trying to escape the realities of the past, the Dorrit family holiday in the fantastical world of Venice that Dickens had dubbed 'An Italian Dream'; both they and David Copperfield take solace in the Swiss Alps that Dickens knew first hand to be a place of escape and recluse. Travel could also be relied upon to add spice and interest to the novel; when the sales of *Martin Chuzzlewit* began to dwindle, Dickens sent his hero to America to win back his audience by trading on the interest aroused in foreign climes.

But moreover, just as travel provided a source of interest in fiction, so too did fiction inspire enthusiasm for travel, not least of all for Dickens. He once wrote that 'When the wind is blowing and the sleet or rain is driving against the dark windows, I love to sit by the fire, thinking of what I have read in books of voyage and travel.' He added that 'such books have had a strong fascination for my mind from my earliest childhood' and we can see in his travels how his love of fiction and adventure influence his perception of the world around him. For Dickens, Verona is the home of Romeo and Juliet, and Shakespeare's language is used throughout to comment upon the sights he sees, just as the *Arabian Nights* are upheld by Dickens throughout his travel writing as a treasure of marvels which the exotic world abroad can only aspire to. Dickens reinforced the relationship between the adventures of the imagination and those we seek out for ourselves through travel. The unimposing nature of Dickens' travel writing, that he had used to avoid controversy, prompted the reader to engage more by querying the validity of opinions which are expressly defined as not being fact. The reader, carried to foreign shores by their mind's eye, were encouraged to make their own observations on the sights before them. For Dickens this travelling of the mind was every bit as valuable as actual holidaying. In 'Some Account of an Extraordinary Traveller' (1850), concerning Mr Booley, a visitor to panoramas in London that depict famous sights of foreign climes, Dickens' description ridicules the character with affection, yet ultimately approves of his attempts to widen his experience of the world through the means available. The panoramas were a gateway to a wider world, otherwise unobtainable to Mr Booley. In just such a way, Dickens, ever the champion of the poor, who could not experience the realities of travel as he did, offered the opportunity through his writings for those who would never travel to have a glimpse of the world beyond their own. As Dickens explains, through Booley,

Some of the best results of actual travel are suggested by such means to those whose lot it is to stay at home. New worlds open out to them, beyond their little worlds, and widen their range of reflection, information, sympathy, and interest. The more man knows of man, the better for the common brotherhood among us all.

– Pete Orford, 2009

On Travel

The Last Cab Driver and the First Omnibus Cad

Of all the cabriolet drivers whom we have ever had the honour and gratification of knowing by sight – and our acquaintance in this way has been most extensive – there is one who made an impression on our mind which can never be effaced, and who awakened in our bosom a feeling of admiration and respect, which we entertain a fatal presentiment will never be called forth again by any human being. He was a man of most simple and prepossessing appearance. He was a brown-whiskered, white-hatted, no-coated cabman; his nose was generally red, and his bright blue eye not unfrequently stood out in bold relief against a black border of artificial workmanship;[1] his boots were of the Wellington form, pulled up to meet his corduroy knee-smalls, or at least to approach as near them as their dimensions would admit of; and his neck was usually garnished with a bright yellow handkerchief. In summer he carried in his mouth a flower; in winter, a straw – slight, but, to a contemplative mind, certain indications of a love of nature, and a taste for botany.

His cabriolet was gorgeously painted – a bright red; and wherever we went, City or West End, Paddington or Holloway, North, East, West, or South, there was the red cab, bumping up against the posts at the street corners, and turning in and out, among hackney coaches, and drays, and carts, and wagons, and omnibuses, and contriving by some strange means or other, to get out of places which no other vehicle but the red cab could ever by any possibility have contrived to get into at all. Our fondness for that red cab was unbounded. How we should have liked to have seen it in the circle at Astley's! Our life upon it, that it should have performed such evolutions as would have put the whole company to shame – Indian chiefs, knights, Swiss peasants, and all.

Some people object to the exertion of getting into cabs, and others object to the difficulty of getting out of them; we think both these are objections which take their rise in perverse and ill-conditioned minds. The getting into a cab is a very pretty and graceful process, which, when well performed, is essentially melodramatic. First, there is the expressive pantomime of every one of the eighteen cabmen on the stand, the moment you raise your eyes from the ground. Then there is your own pantomime in reply – quite a little ballet. Four cabs immediately leave the stand, for your especial accommodation; and the evolutions of the animals who draw them, are beautiful in the extreme, as they grate the wheels of the cabs against the kerbstones, and sport playfully in the kennel. You single out a particular cab, and dart swiftly towards it. One bound, and you are on the first step; turn your body lightly round to the right, and you are on the second; bend gracefully beneath the reins, working round to the left at the same time, and you are in the cab. There is no difficulty in finding a seat: the apron knocks you comfortably into it at once, and off you go.

The getting out of a cab is, perhaps, rather more complicated in its theory, and a shade more difficult in its execution. We have studied the subject a great deal, and we think the best way is to throw yourself out and trust to chance for alighting on your feet. If you make the driver alight first, and then throw yourself upon him, you will find that he breaks your fall materially. In the event of your contemplating an offer of eight pence, on no account make the tender, or show the money, until you are safely on the pavement. It is very bad policy attempting to save the four pence. You are very much in the power of a cabman, and he considers it a kind of fee not to do you any wilful damage. Any instruction, however, in the art of getting out of a cab, is wholly unnecessary if you are going any distance, because the probability is, that you will be shot lightly out before you have completed the third mile.

We are not aware of any instance on record in which a cab horse has performed three consecutive miles without going down once. What of that? It is all excitement. And in these days of derangement of the nervous system and universal lassitude, people are content to pay handsomely for excitement; where can it be procured at a cheaper rate?

But to return to the red cab; it was omnipresent. You had but to walk down Holborn, or Fleet Street, or any of the principal thoroughfares in which there is a great deal of traffic, and judge for yourself. You had hardly turned into the street, when you saw a trunk or two, lying on the ground; an uprooted post, a hatbox, a portmanteau, and a carpetbag, strewed about in a very picturesque manner; a horse in a cab standing by, looking about him with great unconcern; and a crowd, shouting and screaming with delight, cooling their flushed faces against the glass windows of a chemist's shop.

'What's the matter here, can you tell me?'

'O'ny a cab, sir.'

'Anybody hurt, do you know?'

'O'ny the fare, sir. I see him a turnin' the corner, and I ses to another gen'lm'n "that's a reg'lar little oss that, and he's a comin' along rayther sweet, an't he?" "He just is," ses the other gen'lm'n, ven bump they cums agin the post, and out flies the fare like bricks.'

Need we say it was the red cab; or that the gentleman with the straw in his mouth, who emerged so coolly from the chemist's shop and philosophically climbing into the little dickey, started off at full gallop, was the red cab's licensed driver?

The ubiquity of this red cab, and the influence it exercised over the risible muscles of justice itself, was perfectly astonishing. You walked into the justice room of the Mansion House; the whole court resounded with merriment. The Lord Mayor threw himself back in his chair, in a state of frantic delight at his own joke; every vein in Mr Hobler's countenance was swollen with laughter, partly at the Lord Mayor's facetiousness, but more at his own; the constables and police officers were (as in duty bound) in ecstasies at Mr Hobler and the Lord Mayor combined; and the very paupers, glancing respectfully at the beadle's countenance, tried to smile, as even he relaxed. A tall, weazen-faced man, with an impediment in his speech, would be endeavouring to state a case of imposition against the red cab's driver; and the red cab's driver, and the Lord Mayor, and Mr Hobler, would be having a little fun among themselves, to the inordinate delight of everybody but the complainant. In the end, justice would be so tickled with the red cab driver's native humour, that the fine would be mitigated, and he would go away full gallop, in the red cab, to impose on somebody else without loss of time.

The driver of the red cab, confident in the strength of his own moral principles, like many other philosophers, was wont to set the feelings and opinions of society at complete defiance. Generally speaking, perhaps, he would as soon carry a fare safely to his destination, as he would upset him – sooner, perhaps, because in that case he not only got the money, but had the additional amusement of running a longer heat against some smart rival. But society made war upon him in the shape of penalties, and he must make war upon society in his own way. This was the reasoning of the red cab driver. So, he bestowed a searching look upon the fare, as he put his hand in his waistcoat pocket, when he had gone half the mile, to get the money ready; and if he brought forth eight pence, out he went.

The last time we saw our friend was one wet evening in Tottenham Court Road, when he was engaged in a very warm and somewhat personal altercation with a loquacious little gentleman in a green coat. Poor fellow! There were great excuses to be made for him: he had not received above eighteen pence more than his fare, and consequently laboured under a great deal of very natural indignation. The dispute had attained a pretty considerable height, when at last the loquacious little gentleman, making a mental calculation of the distance, and finding that he had already paid more than he ought, avowed his unalterable determination to 'pull up' the cabman in the morning.

'Now, just mark this, young man,' said the little gentleman, 'I'll pull you up tomorrow morning.'

'No! will you though?' said our friend, with a sneer.

'I will,' replied the little gentleman, 'mark my words, that's all. If I live till tomorrow morning, you shall repent this.'

There was a steadiness of purpose, and indignation of speech, about the little gentleman, as he took an angry pinch of snuff, after this last declaration, which made a visible impression on the mind of the red cab driver. He appeared to hesitate for an instant. It was only for an instant; his resolve was soon taken.

'You'll pull me up, will you?' said our friend.

'I will,' rejoined the little gentleman, with even greater vehemence than before.

'Very well,' said our friend, tucking up his shirt sleeves very calmly. 'There'll be three veeks for that. Wery good; that'll bring me up to the middle o' next month. Three veeks more would carry me on to my birthday, and then I've got ten pound to draw. I may as well get board, lodgin', and washin', till then, out of the county, as pay for it myself; consequently here goes!'

So, without more ado, the red cab driver knocked the little gentleman down, and then called the police to take himself into custody, with all the civility in the world.

A story is nothing without the sequel; and therefore, we may state, that to our certain knowledge, the board, lodging, and washing were all provided in due course. We happen to know the fact, for it came to our knowledge thus: we went over the House of Correction for the county of Middlesex shortly after, to witness the operation of the silent system; and looked on all the 'wheels'[2] with the greatest anxiety, in search of our long-lost friend. He was nowhere to be seen, however, and we began to think that the little gentleman in the green coat must have relented, when, as we were traversing the kitchen garden, which lies in a sequestered part of the prison, we were startled by hearing a voice, which apparently proceeded from the wall, pouring forth its soul in the plaintive air of 'All round my hat' which was then just beginning to form a recognised portion of our national music.

We started. 'What voice is that?' said we. The Governor shook his head. 'Sad fellow,' he replied, 'very sad. He positively refused to work on the wheel; so, after many trials, I was compelled to order him into solitary confinement. He says he likes it very much though, and I am afraid he does, for he lies on his back on the floor, and sings comic songs all day!'

Shall we add, that our heart had not deceived us and that the comic singer was no other than our eagerly-sought friend, the red cab driver?

We have never seen him since, but we have strong reason to suspect that this noble individual was a distant relative of a waterman of our acquaintance, who, on one occasion, when we were passing the coach stand over which he presides, after standing very quietly to see a tall man struggle into a cab, ran up very briskly when it was all over (as his brethren invariably do), and, touching his hat, asked, as a matter of course, for 'a copper for the waterman'. Now, the fare was by no means a handsome man; and, waxing very indignant at the demand, he replied, 'Money! What for? Coming up and looking at me, I suppose!'

'Vell, sir,' rejoined the waterman, with a smile of immovable complacency, '*that's* worth two pence.'

The identical waterman afterwards attained a very prominent station in society; and as we know something of his life, and have often thought of telling what we *do* know, perhaps we shall never have a better opportunity than the present.

Mr William Barker, then, for that was the gentleman's name, Mr William Barker was born – but why need we relate where Mr William Barker was born, or when? Why scrutinise the entries in parochial ledgers, or seek to penetrate the Lucilian mysteries of lying-in hospitals?[3] Mr William Barker *was* born, or he had never been. There is a son – there was a father. There

8

is an effect – there was a cause. Surely this is sufficient information for the most Fatima-like curiosity;[4] and, if it be not, we regret our inability to supply any further evidence on the point. Can there be a more satisfactory, or more strictly parliamentary course? Impossible.

We at once avow a similar inability to record at what precise period, or by what particular process, this gentleman's patronymic, of William Barker, became corrupted into 'Bill Boorker'. Mr Barker acquired a high standing, and no inconsiderable reputation, among the members of that profession to which he more peculiarly devoted his energies; and to them he was generally known, either by the familiar appellation of 'Bill Boorker,' or the flattering designation of 'Aggerawatin Bill', the latter being a playful and expressive *sobriquet*, illustrative of Mr Barker's great talent in 'aggerawatin' and rendering wild such subjects of Her Majesty as are conveyed from place to place, through the instrumentality of omnibuses. Of the early life of Mr Barker little is known, and even that little is involved in considerable doubt and obscurity. A want of application, a restlessness of purpose, a thirsting after porter, a love of all that is roving and cadger-like in nature, shared in common with many other great geniuses, appear to have been his leading characteristics. The busy hum of a parochial free-school, and the shady repose of a county gaol, were alike inefficacious in producing the slightest alteration in Mr Barker's disposition. His feverish attachment to change and variety nothing could repress; his native daring no punishment could subdue.

If Mr Barker can be fairly said to have had any weakness in his earlier years, it was an amiable one – love, love in its most comprehensive form – a love of ladies, liquids, and pocket handkerchiefs. It was no selfish feeling; it was not confined to his own possessions, which but too many men regard with exclusive complacency. No, it was a nobler love – a general principle. It extended itself with equal force to the property of other people.

There is something very affecting in this. It is still more affecting to know, that such philanthropy is but imperfectly rewarded. Bow Street, Newgate, and Millbank, are a poor return for general benevolence, evincing itself in an irrepressible love for all created objects. Mr Barker felt it so. After a lengthened interview with the highest legal authorities, he quitted his ungrateful country, with the consent, and at the expense, of its Government; proceeded to a distant shore; and there employed himself, like another Cincinnatus, in clearing and cultivating the soil – a peaceful pursuit, in which a term of seven years glided almost imperceptibly away.

Whether, at the expiration of the period we have just mentioned, the British Government required Mr Barker's presence here, or did not require his residence abroad, we have no distinct means of ascertaining. We should be inclined, however, to favour the latter position, inasmuch as we do not find that he was advanced to any other public post on his return, than the post at the corner of the Haymarket, where he officiated as assistant-waterman to the hackney coach stand. Seated, in this capacity, on a couple of tubs near the Kerbstone, with a brass plate and number suspended round his neck by a massive chain, and his ankles curiously enveloped in haybands, he is supposed to have made those observations on human nature which exercised so material an influence over all his proceedings in later life.

Mr Barker had not officiated for many months in this capacity, when the appearance of the first omnibus caused the public mind to go in a new direction, and prevented a great many hackney coaches from going in any direction at all. The genius of Mr Barker at once perceived the whole extent of the injury that would be eventually inflicted on cab and coach stands, and, by consequence, on watermen also, by the progress of the system of which the first omnibus was a part. He saw, too, the necessity of adopting some more profitable profession; and his active mind at once perceived how much might be done in the way of enticing the youthful and unwary, and shoving the old and helpless, into the wrong bus, and carrying them off, until, reduced to despair, they ransomed themselves by the payment of sixpence a-head, or, to adopt his own figurative expression in all its native beauty, 'till they was rig'larly done over, and forked out the stumpy'.

An opportunity for realising his fondest anticipations, soon presented itself. Rumours were rife on the hackney coach stands, that a bus was building, to run from Lisson Grove to the Bank, down Oxford Street and Holborn; and the rapid increase of buses on the Paddington road, encouraged the idea. Mr Barker secretly and cautiously inquired in the proper quarters. The report was correct; the 'Royal William' was to make its first journey on the following Monday. It was a crack affair altogether. An enterprising young cabman, of established reputation as a dashing whip – for he had compromised with the parents of three scrunched children, and just 'worked out' his fine for knocking down an old lady – was the driver; and the spirited proprietor, knowing Mr Barker's qualifications, appointed him to the vacant office of cad on the very first application. The bus began to run, and Mr Barker entered into a new suit of clothes, and on a new sphere of action.

To recapitulate all the improvements introduced by this extraordinary man into the omnibus system – gradually, indeed, but surely – would occupy a far greater space than we are enabled to devote to this imperfect memoir. To him is universally assigned the original suggestion of the practice which afterwards became so general – of the driver of a second bus keeping constantly behind the first one, and driving the pole of his vehicle either into the door of the other, every time it was opened, or through the body of any lady or gentleman who might make an attempt to get into it; a humorous and pleasant invention, exhibiting all that originality of idea, and fine, bold flow of spirits, so conspicuous in every action of this great man.

Mr Barker had opponents of course; what man in public life has not? But even his worst enemies cannot deny that he has taken more old ladies and gentlemen to Paddington who wanted to go to the Bank, and more old ladies and gentlemen to the Bank who wanted to go to Paddington, than any six men on the road; and however much malevolent spirits may pretend to doubt the accuracy of the statement, they well know it to be an established fact, that he has forcibly conveyed a variety of ancient persons of either sex, to both places, who had not the slightest or most distant intention of going anywhere at all.

Mr Barker was the identical cad who nobly distinguished himself, some time since, by keeping a tradesman on the step – the omnibus going at full speed all the time – till he had thrashed him to his entire satisfaction, and finally throwing him away, when he had quite done with him. Mr Barker it *ought* to have been, who honestly indignant at being ignominiously ejected from a house of public entertainment, kicked the landlord in the knee, and thereby caused his death. We say it *ought* to have been Mr Barker, because the action was not a common one, and could have emanated from no ordinary mind.

It has now become matter of history; it is recorded in the Newgate Calendar; and we wish we could attribute this piece of daring heroism to Mr Barker. We regret being compelled to state that it was not performed by him. Would, for the family credit we could add, that it was achieved by his brother!

It was in the exercise of the nicer details of his profession, that Mr Barker's knowledge of human nature was beautifully displayed. He could tell at a glance where a passenger wanted to go to, and would shout the name of the place accordingly, without the slightest reference to the real destination of the vehicle. He knew exactly the kind of old lady that would be too much flurried by the process of pushing in and pulling out of the caravan, to discover where she had been put down, until too late; had an intuitive perception of what was passing in a passenger's mind when he inwardly resolved to 'pull that cad up tomorrow morning'; and never failed to make himself agreeable to female servants, whom he would place next the door, and talk to all the way.

Human judgment is never infallible, and it would occasionally happen that Mr Barker experimentalised with the timidity or forbearance of the wrong person, in which case a summons to a police office, was, on more than one occasion, followed by a committal to prison. It was not in the power of trifles such as these, however, to subdue the freedom of his spirit. As soon as they passed away, he resumed the duties of his profession with unabated ardour.

We have spoken of Mr Barker and of the red cab driver, in the past tense. Alas! Mr Barker has again become an absentee;[5] and the class of men to which they both belonged is fast disappearing. Improvement has peered beneath the aprons of our cabs, and penetrated to the very innermost recesses of our omnibuses. Dirt and fustian will vanish before cleanliness and livery. Slang will be forgotten when civility becomes general: and that enlightened, eloquent, sage, and profound body, the Magistracy of London, will be deprived of half their amusement, and half their occupation.

The Passage Out

We all dined together that day; and a rather formidable party we were: no fewer than eighty-six strong. The vessel being pretty deep in the water, with all her coals on board and so many passengers, and the weather being calm and quiet, there was but little motion; so that before the dinner was half over, even those passengers who were most distrustful of themselves plucked up amazingly; and those who in the morning had returned to the universal question, 'Are you a good sailor?' a very decided negative, now either parried the inquiry with the evasive reply, 'Oh! I suppose I'm no worse than anybody else'; or, reckless of all moral obligations, answered boldly 'Yes', and with some irritation too, as though they would add, 'I should like to know what you see in *me*, sir, particularly, to justify suspicion!'

Notwithstanding this high tone of courage and confidence, I could not but observe that very few remained long over their wine; and that everybody had an unusual love of the open air; and that the favourite and most coveted seats were invariably those nearest to the door. The tea table, too, was by no means as well attended as the dinner table; and there was less whist playing than might have been expected. Still, with the exception of one lady, who had retired with some precipitation at dinner-time, immediately after being assisted to the finest cut of a very yellow boiled leg of mutton with very green capers, there were no invalids as yet; and walking, and smoking, and drinking of brandy-and-water (but always in the open air), went on with unabated spirit, until eleven o'clock or thereabouts, when 'turning in' – no sailor of seven hours' experience talks of going to bed – became the order of the night. The perpetual tramp of boot heels on the decks gave place to a heavy silence, and the whole human freight was stowed away below, excepting a very few stragglers, like myself, who were probably, like me, afraid to go there.

To one unaccustomed to such scenes, this is a very striking time on shipboard. Afterwards, and when its novelty had long worn off, it never ceased to have a peculiar interest and charm for me. The gloom through which the great black mass holds its direct and certain course; the rushing water, plainly heard, but dimly seen; the broad, white, glistening track, that follows in the vessel's wake; the men on the lookout forward, who would be scarcely visible against the dark sky, but for their blotting out some score of glistening stars; the helmsman at the wheel, with the illuminated card before him, shining, a speck of light amidst the darkness, like something sentient and of divine intelligence; the melancholy sighing of the wind through block, and rope, and chain; the gleaming forth of light from every crevice, nook, and tiny piece of glass about the decks, as though the ship were filled with fire in hiding, ready to burst through any outlet, wild with its resistless power of death and ruin. At first, too, and even when the hour, and all the objects it exalts, have come to be familiar, it is difficult, alone and thoughtful, to hold them to their proper shapes and forms. They change with the wandering fancy; assume the semblance of things left far away; put on the well-remembered aspect of favourite places dearly loved; and even people them with shadows. Streets, houses, rooms; figures so like their usual occupants, that they have startled me by their reality, which far exceeded, as it seemed to me, all power of mine to conjure up the absent; have, many and many a time, at such an hour, grown suddenly out of objects with whose real look, and use, and purpose, I was as well acquainted as with my own two hands.

My own two hands, and feet likewise, being very cold, how-ever, on this particular occasion, I crept below at midnight. It was not exactly comfortable below. It was decidedly close; and it was impossible to be unconscious of the presence of that extraordinary compound of strange smells, which is to be found nowhere but on board ship, and which is such a subtle perfume that it seems to enter at every pore of the skin, and whisper of the hold. Two passengers' wives (one of them my own) lay already in silent agonies on the sofa; and one lady's maid (*my* lady's) was a mere bundle on the floor, execrating her destiny, and pounding her curlpapers among the stray boxes. Everything sloped the wrong way: which in itself was an aggravation scarcely to be borne. I had left the door open, a moment before, in the bosom of a gentle declivity, and, when I turned to shut it, it was on the summit of a lofty eminence. Now every plank and timber creaked, as if the ship were made of wickerwork; and now crackled, like an enormous fire of the driest possible twigs. There was nothing for it but bed; so I went to bed.

It was pretty much the same for the next two days, with a tolerably fair wind and dry weather. I read in bed (but to this hour I don't know what) a good deal; and reeled on deck a little; drank cold brandy-and-water with an unspeakable disgust, and ate hard biscuit perseveringly: not ill, but going to be.

It is the third morning. I am awakened out of my sleep by a dismal shriek from my wife, who demands to know whether there's any danger. I rouse myself, and look out of bed. The water jug is plunging and leaping like a lively dolphin; all the smaller articles are afloat, except my shoes, which are stranded on a carpet-bag, high and dry, like a couple of coal barges. Suddenly I see them spring into the air, and behold the looking glass, which is nailed to the wall, sticking fast upon the ceiling. At the same time the door entirely disappears, and a new one is opened in the floor. Then I begin to comprehend that the stateroom is standing on its head.

Before it is possible to make any arrangement at all compatible with this novel state of things, the ship rights. Before one can say 'Thank Heaven!', she wrongs again. Before one can cry she *is* wrong, she seems to have started forward, and to be a creature actually running of its own accord, with broken knees and failing legs, through every variety of hole and pitfall, and stumbling constantly. Before one can so much as wonder, she takes a high leap into the air. Before she has well done that, she takes a deep dive into the water. Before she has gained the surface, she throws a somersault. The instant she is on her legs, she rushes backward. And so she goes on staggering, heaving, wrestling, leaping, diving, jumping, pitching, throbbing, rolling, and rocking: and going through all these movements, sometimes by turns, and sometimes altogether: until one feels disposed to roar for mercy.

A steward passes. 'Steward!'

'Sir?'

'What *is* the matter? What *do* you call this?'

'Rather a heavy sea on, sir, and a headwind.'

A headwind! Imagine a human face upon the vessel's prow, with fifteen thousand Sampsons in one bent upon driving her back, and hitting her exactly between the eyes whenever she attempts to advance an inch. Imagine the ship herself, with every pulse and artery of her huge body swollen and bursting under this maltreatment, sworn to go on or die. Imagine the wind howling, the sea roaring, the rain beating: all in furious array against her. Picture the sky both dark and wild, and the clouds, in fearful sympathy with the waves, making another ocean in the air. Add to all this, the clattering on deck and down below; the tread of hurried feet; the loud hoarse shouts of seamen; the gurgling in and out of water through the scuppers; with, every now and then, the striking of a heavy sea upon the planks above, with the deep, dead, heavy sound of thunder heard within a vault – and there is the headwind of that January morning.

I say nothing of what may be called the domestic noises of the ship: such as the breaking of glass and crockery, the tumbling down of stewards, the gambols, overhead, of loose casks and truant dozens of bottled porter, and the very remarkable and far from exhilarating sounds raised in their various staterooms by the seventy passengers who were too ill to get up to breakfast. I say nothing of them: for although I lay listening to this concert for three or four days, I don't think I heard it for more than a quarter of a minute, at the expiration of which term, I lay down again, excessively seasick.

Not seasick, be it understood, in the ordinary acceptation of the term – I wish I had been – but in a form which I have never seen or heard described, though I have no doubt it is very common. I lay there, all the day long, quite coolly and contentedly; with no sense of weariness, with no desire to get up, or get better, or take the air; with no curiosity, or care, or regret, of any sort or degree, saving that I think I can remember, in this universal indifference, having a kind of lazy joy – of fiendish delight, if anything so lethargic can be dignified with the title – in the fact of my wife being too ill to talk to me. If I may be allowed to illustrate my state of mind by such an example, I should say that I was exactly in the condition of the elder Mr Willet, after the incursion of the rioters into his bar at Chigwell.[6] Nothing would have surprised me. If, in the momentary illumination of any ray of intelligence that may have come upon me in the way of thoughts of home, a goblin postman, with a scarlet coat and bell, had come into that little kennel before me, broad awake in broad day, and, apologising for being damp through walking in the sea, had handed me a letter directed to myself, in familiar characters, I am certain I should not have felt one atom of astonishment: I should have been perfectly satisfied. If Neptune himself had walked in, with a toasted shark on his trident, I should have looked upon the event as one of the very commonest everyday occurrences.

Once – once – I found myself on deck. I don't know how I got there, or what possessed me to go there, but there I was; and completely dressed too, with a huge pea coat on, and a pair of boots such as no weak man in his senses could ever have got into. I found myself standing, when a gleam of consciousness came upon me, holding on to something. I don't know what. I think it was the boatswain: or it may have been the pump: or possibly the cow. I can't say how long I had been there; whether a day or a minute. I recollect trying to think about something (about anything in the whole wide world, I was not particular) without the smallest effect. I could not even make out which was the sea, and which the sky, for the horizon seemed drunk, and was flying wildly about in all directions. Even in that incapable state, however, I recognised the lazy gentleman[7] standing before me: nautically clad in a suit of shaggy blue, with an oilskin hat. But I was too imbecile, although I knew it to be he, to separate him from his dress; and tried to call him, I remember, *Pilot*. After another interval of total unconsciousness, I found he had gone, and recognised another figure in its place. It seemed to wave and fluctuate before me as though I saw it reflected in an unsteady looking glass; but I knew it for the captain; and such was the cheerful influence of his face, that I tried to smile: yes, even then I tried to smile. I saw by his gestures that he addressed me; but it was a long time before I could make out that he remonstrated against my standing up to my knees in water – as I was; of course I don't know why. I tried to thank him, but couldn't. I could only point to my boots – or wherever I supposed my boots to be – and say in a plaintive voice, 'Cork soles': at the same time endeavouring, I am told, to sit down in the pool. Finding that I was quite insensible, and for the time a maniac, he humanely conducted me below.

There I remained until I got better: suffering, whenever I was recommended to eat anything, an amount of anguish only second to that which is said to be endured by the apparently drowned, in the process of restoration to life. One gentleman on board had a letter of introduction to me from a mutual friend in London. He sent it below with his card, on the morning of the headwind; and I was long troubled with the idea that he might be up, and well, and a hundred times a day expecting me to call upon him in the saloon. I imagined him one of those cast-iron images – I will not call them men – who ask, with red faces, and lusty voices, what seasickness means, and whether it really is as bad as it is represented to be. This was very torturing indeed; and I don't think I ever felt such perfect gratification and gratitude of heart, as I did when I heard from the ship's doctor that he had been obliged to put a large mustard poultice on this very gentleman's stomach.[8] I date my recovery from the receipt of that intelligence.

It was materially assisted though, I have no doubt, by a heavy gale of wind, which came slowly up at sunset, when we were about ten days out, and raged with gradually increasing fury until morning, saving that it lulled for an hour a little before midnight. There was something in the unnatural repose of that hour, and in the after-gathering of the storm, so inconceivably awful and tremendous, that its bursting into full violence was almost a relief.

The labouring of the ship in the troubled sea on this night I shall never forget. 'Will it ever be worse than this?' was a question I had often heard asked, when everything was sliding and bumping about, and when it certainly did seem difficult to comprehend the possibility of anything afloat being more disturbed, without toppling over and going down. But what the agitation of a steam vessel is, on a bad winter's night in the wild Atlantic, it is impossible for the most vivid imagination to conceive. To say that she is flung down on her side in the waves, with her masts dipping into them, and that, springing up again, she rolls over on the other side, until a heavy sea strikes her with the noise of a hundred great guns, and hurls her back – that she stops, and staggers, and shivers, as though stunned, and then, with a violent throbbing at her heart, darts onward like a monster goaded into madness, to be beaten down, and battered, and crushed, and leaped on by the angry sea – that thunder, lightning, hail, and rain, and wind, are all in fierce contention for the mastery – that every plank has its groan, every nail its shriek, and every drop of water in the great ocean its howling voice – is nothing. To say that all is grand, and all appalling and horrible in the last degree, is nothing. Words cannot express it. Thoughts cannot convey it. Only a dream can call it up again, in all its fury, rage, and passion.

And yet, in the very midst of these terrors, I was placed in a situation so exquisitely ridiculous, that even then I had as strong a sense of its absurdity as I have now, and could no more help laughing than I can at any other comical incident, happening under circumstances the most favourable to its enjoyment. About midnight we shipped a sea, which forced its way through the skylights, burst open the doors above, and came raging and roaring down into the ladies' cabin, to the unspeakable consternation of my wife and a little Scotch lady – who, by the way, had previously sent a message to the captain by the stewardess, requesting him, with her compliments, to have a steel conductor immediately attached to the top of every mast, and to the chimney, in order that the ship might not be struck by lightning. They and the handmaid before mentioned, being in such ecstasies of fear that I scarcely knew what to do with them, I naturally bethought myself of some restorative or comfortable cordial; and nothing better occurring to me, at the moment, than hot brandy-and-water, I procured a tumbler full without delay. It being impossible to stand or sit without holding on, they were all heaped together in one corner of a long sofa – a fixture extending entirely across the cabin – where they clung to each other in momentary expectation of being drowned. When I approached this place with my specific, and was about to administer it with many consolatory expressions to the nearest sufferer, what was my dismay to see them all roll slowly down to the other end! And when I staggered to that end, and held out the glass once more, how immensely baffled were my good intentions by the ship giving another lurch, and their all rolling back again! I suppose I dodged them up and down this sofa for at least a quarter of an hour, without reaching them once; and by the time I did catch them, the brandy-and-water was diminished, by constant spilling, to a teaspoonful. To complete the group, it is necessary to recognise in this disconcerted dodger, an individual very pale from seasickness, who had shaved his beard and brushed his hair, last, at Liverpool: and whose only article of dress (linen not included) were a pair of dreadnought trousers; a blue jacket, formerly admired upon the Thames at Richmond; no stockings; and one slipper.

Of the outrageous antics performed by that ship next morning; which made bed a practical joke, and getting up, by any process short of falling out, an impossibility; I say nothing. But anything like the utter dreariness and desolation that met my eyes when I literally 'tumbled up' on deck at noon, I never saw. Ocean and sky were all of one dull, heavy, uniform, lead colour. There was no extent of prospect even over the dreary waste that lay around us, for the sea ran high, and the horizon encompassed us like a large black hoop. Viewed from the air, or some tall bluff on shore, it would have been imposing and stupendous, no doubt; but seen from the wet and rolling decks, it only impressed one giddily and painfully. In the gale of last night the lifeboat had been crushed by one blow of the sea like a walnut shell; and there it hung dangling in the air: a mere faggot of crazy boards. The planking of the paddle-boxes had been torn sheer away. The wheels were exposed and bare; and they whirled and dashed their spray about the decks at random. Chimney, white with crusted salt; topmasts struck; storm sails set; rigging all knotted, tangled, wet, and drooping: a gloomier picture it would be hard to look upon.

I was now comfortably established by courtesy in the ladies' cabin, where, besides ourselves, there were only four other passengers. First, the little Scotch lady before-mentioned, on her way to join her husband at New York, who had settled there three years before. Secondly and thirdly, an honest young Yorkshireman, connected with some American house; domiciled in that same city, and carrying thither his beautiful young wife to whom he had been married but a fortnight, and who was the fairest specimen of a comely English country girl I have ever seen. Fourthly, fifthly, and lastly, another couple – newly married too, if one might judge from the endearments they frequently interchanged – of whom I know no more than that they were rather a mysterious, runaway kind of couple; that the lady had great personal attractions also; and that the gentleman carried more guns with him than Robinson Crusoe, wore a shooting coat, and had two great dogs on board. On further consideration, I remember that he tried hot roast pig and bottled ale as a cure for seasickness; and that he took these remedies (usually in bed) day after day, with astonishing perseverance. I may add, for the information of the curious, that they decidedly failed.

The weather continuing obstinately and almost unpreced-entedly bad, we usually straggled into this cabin, more or less faint and miserable, about an hour before noon, and lay down on the sofas to recover; during which interval, the captain would look in to communicate the state of the wind, the moral certainty of its changing tomorrow (the weather is always going to improve tomorrow, at sea), the vessel's rate of sailing, and so forth. Observations there were none to tell us of, for there was no sun to take them by. But a description of one day will serve for all the rest. Here it is.

The captain being gone, we compose ourselves to read, if the place be light enough; and if not, we doze and talk altern-ately. At one, a bell rings, and the stewardess comes down with a steaming dish of baked potatoes, and another of roasted apples; and plates of pig's face, cold ham, salt beef; or perhaps a smoking mess of rare hot collops. We fall to upon these dainties; eat as much as we can (we have great appetites now); and are as long as possible about it. If the fire will burn (it *will* sometimes) we are pretty cheerful. If it won't, we all remark to each other that it's very cold, rub our hands, cover ourselves with coats and cloaks, and lie down again to doze, talk, and read (provided as aforesaid), until dinnertime. At five, another bell rings, and the stewardess reappears with another dish of potatoes – boiled this time – and store of hot meat of various kinds, not forgetting the roast pig, to be taken medicinally. We sit down at table again (rather more cheerfully than before); prolong the meal with a rather mouldy dessert of apples, grapes, and oranges; and drink our wine and brandy-and-water. The bottles and glasses are still upon the table, and the oranges and so forth are rolling about according to their fancy and the ship's way, when the doctor comes down, by special nightly invitation, to join our evening rubber, imme-diately on whose arrival we make a party at whist, and as it is a rough night and the cards will not lie on the cloth, we put the tricks in our pockets as we take them. At whist we remain with exemplary gravity (deducting a short time for tea and toast) until eleven o'clock, or thereabouts; when the captain comes down again, in a sou'-wester hat tied under his chin, and a pilot coat, making the ground wet where he stands. By this time the card playing is over, and the bottles and glasses are again upon the table; and after an hour's pleasant conversation about the ship, the passengers, and things in general, the captain (who never goes to bed, and is never out of humour) turns up his coat collar for the deck again; shakes hands all round; and goes laughing out into the weather as merrily as to a birthday party.

As to daily news, there is no dearth of that commodity. This passenger is reported to have lost fourteen pounds at *vingt-et-un* in the saloon yesterday; and that passenger drinks his bottle of champagne every day, and how he does it (being only a clerk), nobody knows. The head engineer has distinctly said that there never was such times – meaning weather – and four good hands are ill, and have given in, deadbeat. Several berths are full of water, and all the cabins are leaky. The ship's cook, secretly swigging damaged whisky, has been found drunk; and has been played upon by the fire engine[9] until quite sober. All the stewards have fallen downstairs at various dinnertimes, and go about with plasters in various places. The baker is ill, and so is the pastry cook. A new man, horribly indisposed, has been required to fill the place of the latter officer; and has been propped and jammed up with empty casks in a little house upon deck, and commanded to roll out piecrust, which he protests (being highly bilious) it is death to him to look at. News! A dozen murders on shore would lack the interest of these slight incidents at sea.

Divided between our rubber and such topics as these, we were running (as we thought) into Halifax Harbour, on the fifteenth night, with little wind and a bright moon – indeed, we had made the light at its outer entrance, and put the pilot in charge – when suddenly the ship struck upon a bank of mud. An immediate rush on deck took place of course; the sides were crowded in an instant; and for a few minutes we were in as lively a state of confusion as the greatest lover of disorder would desire to see. The passengers, and guns, and water casks, and other heavy matters, being all huddled together aft, however, to lighten her in the head, she was soon got off; and after some driving on towards an uncomfortable line of objects (whose vicinity had been announced very early in the disaster by a loud cry of 'Breakers ahead!') and much backing of paddles, and heaving of the lead into a constantly decreasing depth of water, we dropped anchor in a strange outlandish-looking nook which nobody on board could recognise, although there was land all about us, and so close that we could plainly see the waving branches of the trees.

It was strange enough, in the silence of midnight, and the dead stillness that seemed to be created by the sudden and un-expected stoppage of the engine which had been clanking and blasting in our ears incessantly for so many days, to watch the look of blank astonishment expressed in every face, beginning with the officers, tracing it through all the passengers, and descending to the very stokers and furnace men, who emerged from below, one by one, and clustered together in a smoky group about the hatchway of the engine room, comparing notes in whispers. After throwing up a few rockets and firing signal guns in the hope of being hailed from the land, or at least of seeing a light – but without any other sight or sound presenting itself – it was determined to send a boat on shore. It was amusing to observe how very kind some of the passengers were, in volunteering to go ashore in this same boat – for the general good, of course – not by any means because they thought the ship in an unsafe position, or contemplated the possibility of her heeling over in case the tide were running out. Nor was it less amusing to remark how desperately unpopular the poor pilot became in one short minute. He had had his passage out from Liverpool, and during the whole voyage had been quite a notorious character, as a teller of anecdotes and cracker of jokes. Yet here were the very men who had laughed the loudest at his jests, now flourishing their fists in his face, loading him with imprecations, and defying him to his teeth as a villain!

The boat soon shoved off, with a lantern and sundry blue lights on board; and in less than an hour returned; the officer in command bringing with him a tolerably tall young tree, which he had plucked up by the roots, to satisfy certain distrustful passengers whose minds misgave them that they were to be imposed upon and shipwrecked, and who would on no other terms believe that he had been ashore, or had done anything but fraudulently row a little way into the mist, specially to deceive them and compass their deaths. Our captain had fore-seen from the first that we must be in a place called the Eastern Passage; and so we were. It was about the last place in the world in which we had any business or reason to be, but a sudden fog, and some error on the pilot's part, were the cause. We were surrounded by banks, and rocks, and shoals of all kinds, but had happily drifted, it seemed, upon the only safe speck that was to be found thereabouts. Eased by this report, and by the assurance that the tide was past the ebb, we turned in at three o'clock in the morning.

I was dressing about half-past nine next day, when the noise above hurried me on deck. When I had left it overnight, it was dark, foggy, and damp, and there were bleak hills all round us. Now, we were gliding down a smooth, broad stream, at the rate of eleven miles an hour: our colours flying gaily; our crew rigged out in their smartest clothes; our officers in uniform again; the sun shining as on a brilliant April day in England; the land stretched out on either side, streaked with light patches of snow; white wooden houses; people at their doors; telegraphs working; flags hoisted; wharfs appearing; ships; quays crowded with people; distant noises; shouts; men and boys running down steep places towards the pier: all more bright and gay and fresh to our unused eyes than words can paint them. We came to a wharf, paved with uplifted faces; got alongside, and were made fast, after some shouting and straining of cables; darted, a score of us along the gangway, almost as soon as it was thrust out to meet us, and before it had reached the ship – and leaped upon the firm glad earth again!

I suppose this Halifax would have appeared an Elysium, though it had been a curiosity of ugly dullness. But I carried away with me a most pleasant impression of the town and its inhabitants, and have preserved it to this hour. Nor was it without regret that I came home, without having found an opportunity of returning thither, and once more shaking hands with the friends I made that day.

It happened to be the opening of the Legislative Council and General Assembly, at which ceremonial the forms observed on the commencement of a new session of parliament in England were so closely copied, and so gravely presented on a small scale, that it was like looking at Westminster through the wrong end of a telescope. The governor, as her Majesty's representative, delivered what may be called the speech from the throne. He said what he had to say manfully and well. The military band outside the building struck up 'God save the Queen' with great vigour before his Excellency had quite finished; the people shouted; the ins rubbed their hands; the outs shook their heads; the government party said there never was such a good speech; the opposition declared there never was such a bad one; the speaker and members of the House of Assembly withdrew from the bar to say a great deal among themselves and do a little, and, in short, everything went on, and promised to go on, just as it does at home upon the like occasions.

The town is built on the side of a hill, the highest point being commanded by a strong fortress, not yet quite finished. Several streets of good breadth and appearance extend from its summit to the waterside, and are intersected by cross streets running parallel with the river. The houses are chiefly of wood. The market is abundantly supplied; and provisions are exceedingly cheap. The weather being unusually mild at that time for the season of the year, there was no sleighing, but there were plenty of those vehicles in yards and by-places, and some of them, from the gorgeous quality of their decorations, might have 'gone on' without alteration as triumphal cars in a melodrama at Astley's. The day was uncommonly fine; the air bracing and healthful; the whole aspect of the town cheerful, thriving, and industrious.

We lay there seven hours, to deliver and exchange the mails. At length, having collected all our bags and all our passengers (including two or three choice spirits, who, having indulged too freely in oysters and champagne, were found lying insensible on their backs in unfrequented streets), the engines were again put in motion, and we stood off for Boston.

Encountering squally weather again in the Bay of Fundy, we tumbled and rolled about as usual all that night and all next day. On the next afternoon, that is to say, on Saturday, the twenty-second of January, an American pilot boat came alongside, and soon afterwards the Britannia steam packet, from Liverpool, eighteen days out, was telegraphed at Boston.

The indescribable interest with which I strained my eyes, as the first patches of American soil peeped like molehills from the green sea, and followed them, as they swelled, by slow and almost imperceptible degrees, into a continuous line of coast, can hardly be exaggerated. A sharp keen wind blew dead against us; a hard frost prevailed on shore; and the cold was most severe. Yet the air was so intensely clear, and dry, and bright, that the temperature was not only endurable, but delicious.

How I remained on deck, staring about me, until we came alongside the dock, and how, though I had had as many eyes as Argus, I should have had them all wide open, and all employed on new objects – are topics which I will not prolong this chapter to discuss. Neither will I more than hint at my foreigner-like mistake in supposing that a party of most active persons, who scrambled on board at the peril of their lives as we approached the wharf, were newsmen, answering to that industrious class at home; whereas, despite the leathern wallets of news slung about the necks of some, and the broad sheets in the hands of all, they were editors, who boarded ships in person (as one gentleman in a worsted comforter informed me), 'because they liked the excitement of it'. Suffice it in this place to say, that one of these invaders, with a ready courtesy for which I thank him here most gratefully, went on before to order rooms at the hotel; and that when I followed, as I soon did, I found myself rolling through the long passages with an involuntary imitation of the gait of Mr T. P. Cooke, in a new nautical melodrama.[10]

'Dinner, if you please,' said I to the waiter.

'When?' said the waiter.

'As quick as possible,' said I.

'Right away?' said the waiter.

After a moment's hesitation, I answered, 'No,' at hazard.

'*Not* right away?' cried the waiter, with an amount of surprise that made me start.

I looked at him doubtfully, and returned, 'No; I would rather have it in this private room. I like it very much.'

At this, I really thought the waiter must have gone out of his mind: as I believe he would have done, but for the interposition of another man, who whispered in his ear, 'Directly'.

'Well! and that's a fact!' said the waiter, looking helplessly at me: 'Right away.'

I saw now that 'right away' and 'directly' were one and the same thing. So I reversed my previous answer, and sat down to dinner in ten minutes afterwards; and a capital dinner it was.

The hotel (a very excellent one) is called the Tremont House. It has more galleries, colonnades, piazzas, and passages than I can remember, or the reader would believe; and is some trifle smaller than Bedford Square.

By Verona, Mantua and Milan, Across the Pass of the Simplon into Switzerland

I had been half afraid to go to Verona, lest it should at all put me out of conceit with *Romeo and Juliet*. But, I was no sooner come into the old marketplace, than the misgiving vanished. It is so fanciful, quaint, and picturesque a place, formed by such an extraordinary and rich variety of fantastic buildings, that there could be nothing better at the core of even this romantic town, scene of one of the most romantic and beautiful of stories.

It was natural enough, to go straight from the marketplace, to the House of the Capulets, now degenerated into a most miserable little inn. Noisy vetturini[11] and muddy market carts were disputing possession of the yard, which was ankle-deep in dirt, with a brood of splashed and bespattered geese; and there was a grim-visaged dog, viciously panting in a doorway, who would certainly have had Romeo by the leg the moment he put it over the wall, if he had existed and been at large in those times. The orchard fell into other hands, and was parted off many years ago; but there used to be one attached to the house – or at all events there may have been – and the hat (Cappêllo) the ancient cognizance of the family, may still be seen, carved in stone, over the gateway of the yard. The geese, the market carts, their drivers, and the dog, were somewhat in the way of the story, it must be confessed; and it would have been pleasanter to have found the house empty, and to have been able to walk through the disused rooms. But the hat was unspeakably comfortable; and the place where the garden used to be, hardly less so. Besides, the house is a distrustful, jealous-looking house as one would desire to see, though of a very moderate size. So I was quite satisfied with it, as the veritable mansion of old Capulet, and was correspondingly grateful in my acknowledgments to an extremely unsentimental middle-aged lady, the Padrona of the Hotel, who was lounging on the threshold looking at the geese; and who at least resembled the Capulets in the one particular of being very great indeed in the 'family' way.

From Juliet's home, to Juliet's tomb, is a transition as natural to the visitor, as to fair Juliet herself, or to the proudest Juliet that ever has taught the torches to burn bright in any time.[12] So, I went off, with a guide, to an old, old garden, once belonging to an old, old convent, I suppose; and being admitted, at a shattered gate, by a bright-eyed woman who was washing clothes, went down some walks where fresh plants and young flowers were prettily growing among fragments of old wall, and ivy-coloured mounds; and was shown a little tank, or water trough, which the bright-eyed woman – drying her arms upon her 'kerchief, called 'La tomba di Giulietta la sfortunáta'.[13] With the best disposition in the world to believe, I could do no more than believe that the bright-eyed woman believed; so I gave her that much credit, and her customary fee in ready money. It was a pleasure, rather than a disappointment, that Juliet's resting place was forgotten. However consolatory it may have been to Yorick's Ghost, to hear the feet upon the pavement overhead, and, twenty times a day, the repetition of his name,[14] it is better for Juliet to lie out of the track of tourists, and to have no visitors but such as come to graves in spring rain, and sweet air, and sunshine.

Pleasant Verona! With its beautiful old palaces, and charming country in the distance, seen from terrace walks, and stately, balustraded galleries. With its Roman gates, still spanning the fair street, and casting, on the sunlight of today, the shade of fifteen hundred years ago. With its marble-fitted churches, lofty towers, rich architecture, and quaint old quiet thoroughfares, where shouts of Montagues and Capulets once resounded,

> And made Verona's ancient citizens
> Cast by their grave, beseeming ornaments,
> To wield old partizans.[15]

With its fast-rushing river, picturesque old bridge, great castle, waving cypresses, and prospect so delightful, and so cheerful! Pleasant Verona!

In the midst of it, in the Piazza di Brá – a spirit of old time among the familiar realities of the passing hour – is the great Roman amphitheatre. So well preserved, and carefully maintained, that every row of seats is there, unbroken. Over certain of the arches, the old Roman numerals may yet be seen; and there are corridors, and staircases, and subterranean passages for beasts, and winding ways, above ground and below, as when the fierce thousands hurried in and out, intent upon the bloody shows of the arena. Nestling in some of the shadows and hollow places of the walls, now, are smiths with their forges, and a few small dealers of one kind or other; and there are green weeds, and leaves, and grass, upon the parapet. But little else is greatly changed.

When I had traversed all about it, with great interest, and had gone up to the topmost round of seats, and turning from the lovely panorama closed in by the distant Alps, looked down into the building, it seemed to lie before me like the inside of a prodigious hat of plaited straw, with an enormously broad brim and a shallow crown; the plaits being represented by the four-and-forty rows of seats. The comparison is a homely and fantastic one, in sober remembrance and on paper, but it was irresistibly suggested at the moment, nevertheless.

An equestrian troop had been there, a short time before – the same troop, I dare say, that appeared to the old lady in the church at Modena – and had scooped out a little ring at one end of the arena; where their performances had taken place, and where the marks of their horses' feet were still fresh. I could not but picture to myself, a handful of spectators gathered together on one or two of the old stone seats, and a spangled cavalier being gallant, or a policinello funny, with the grim walls looking on. Above all, I thought how strangely those Roman mutes would gaze upon the favourite comic scene of the travelling

English, where a British nobleman (Lord John), with a very loose stomach, dressed in a blue-tailed coat down to his heels, bright yellow breeches, and a white hat, comes abroad, riding double on a rearing horse, with an English lady (Lady Betsy) in a straw bonnet and green veil, and a red spencer; and who always carries a gigantic reticule, and a put-up parasol.

I walked through and through the town all the rest of the day, and could have walked there until now, I think. In one place, there was a very pretty modern theatre, where they had just performed the opera (always popular in Verona) of *Romeo and Juliet*. In another there was a collection, under a colonnade, of Greek, Roman, and Etruscan remains, presided over by an ancient man who might have been an Etruscan relic himself; for he was not strong enough to open the iron gate, when he had unlocked it, and had neither voice enough to be audible when he described the curiosities, nor sight enough to see them: he was so very old. In another place, there was a gallery of pictures, so abominably bad, that it was quite delightful to see them mouldering away. But anywhere, in the churches, among the palaces, in the streets, on the bridge, or down beside the river, it was always pleasant Verona, and in my remembrance always will be.

I read *Romeo and Juliet* in my own room at the inn that night – of course, no Englishman had ever read it there, before – and set out for Mantua next day at sunrise, repeating to myself (in the coupé of an omnibus, and next to the conductor, who was reading the Mysteries of Paris),

> There is no world without Verona's walls
> But purgatory, torture, hell itself.
> Hence-banished is banished from the world,
> And world's exile is death.[16]

which reminded me that Romeo was only banished five-and-twenty miles after all, and rather disturbed my confidence in his energy and boldness.

Was the way to Mantua as beautiful, in his time, I wonder? Did it wind through pasture land as green, bright with the same glancing streams, and dotted with fresh clumps of graceful trees? Those purple mountains lay on the horizon, then, for certain; and the dresses of these peasant girls, who wear a great, knobbed, silver pin like an English 'life-preserver' through their hair behind, can hardly be much changed. The hopeful feeling of so bright a morning, and so exquisite a sunrise, can have been no stranger, even to an exiled lover's breast; and Mantua itself must have broken on him in the prospect, with its towers, and walls, and water, pretty much as on a commonplace and matrimonial omnibus. He made the same sharp twists and turns, perhaps, over two rumbling drawbridges; passed through the like long, covered, wooden bridge; and leaving the marshy water behind, approached the rusty gate of stagnant Mantua.

If ever a man were suited to his place of residence, and his place of residence to him, the lean Apothecary and Mantua came together in a perfect fitness of things.[17] It may have been more stirring then, perhaps. If so, the Apothecary was a man in advance of his time, and knew what Mantua would be, in eighteen hundred and forty-four. He fasted much, and that assisted him in his foreknowledge.

I put up at the hotel of the Golden Lion, and was in my own room arranging plans with the Brave Courier,[18] when there came a modest little tap at the door, which opened on an outer gallery surrounding a courtyard; and an intensely shabby little man looked in, to inquire if the gentleman would have a cicerone to show the town. His face was so very wistful and anxious, in the half-opened doorway, and there was so much poverty expressed in his faded suit and little pinched hat, and in the threadbare worsted glove with which he held it – not expressed the less, because these were evidently his genteel clothes, hastily slipped on – that I would as soon have trodden on him as dismissed him. I engaged him on the instant, and he stepped in directly.

While I finished the discussion in which I was engaged, he stood, beaming by himself in a corner, making a feint of brushing my hat with his arm. If his fee had been as many napoleons as it was francs, there could not have shot over the twilight of his shabbiness such a gleam of sun, as lighted up the whole man, now that he was hired.

'Well!' said I, when I was ready, 'shall we go out now?'

'If the gentleman pleases. It is a beautiful day. A little fresh, but charming; altogether charming. The gentleman will allow me to open the door. This is the inn yard. The courtyard of the Golden Lion! The gentleman will please to mind his footing on the stairs.'

We were now in the street.

'This is the street of the Golden Lion. This, the outside of the Golden Lion. The interesting window up there, on the first piano, where the pane of glass is broken, is the window of the gentleman's chamber!'

Having viewed all these remarkable objects, I inquired if there were much to see in Mantua.

'Well! Truly, no. Not much! So, so,' he said, shrugging his shoulders apologetically.

'Many churches?'

'No. Nearly all suppressed by the French.'

'Monasteries or convents?'

'No. The French again! Nearly all suppressed by Napoleon.'

'Much business?'

'Very little business.'

'Many strangers?'

'Ah Heaven!'

I thought he would have fainted.

'Then, when we have seen the two large churches yonder, what shall we do next?' said I.

He looked up the street, and down the street, and rubbed his chin timidly; and then said, glancing in my face as if a light had broken on his mind, yet with a humble appeal to my forbearance that was perfectly irresistible,

'We can take a little turn about the town, Signore!' (Si può far 'un píccolo gíro della citta.)

It was impossible to be anything but delighted with the proposal, so we set off together in great good humour. In the relief of his mind, he opened his heart, and gave up as much of Mantua as a cicerone could.

'One must eat,' he said; 'but, bah! it was a dull place, without doubt!'

He made as much as possible of the Basilica of Santa Andrea – a noble church – and of an enclosed portion of the pavement, about which tapers were burning, and a few people kneeling, and under which is said to be preserved the Sangreal of the old romances. This church disposed of, and another after it (the cathedral of San Pietro), we went to the Museum, which was shut up. 'It was all the same,' he said; 'Bah! There was not much inside!' Then, we went to see the Piazza del Diavolo, built by the Devil (for no particular purpose) in a single night; then, the Piazza Virgiliana; then, the statue of Virgil – *our* poet, my little friend said, plucking up a spirit, for the moment, and putting his hat a little on one side. Then, we went to a dismal sort of farmyard, by which a picture gallery was approached. The moment the gate of this retreat was opened, some five hundred geese came waddling round us, stretching out their necks, and clamouring in the most hideous manner, as if they were ejaculating, 'Oh! here's somebody come to see the pictures! Don't go up! Don't go up!' While we went up, they waited very quietly about the door in a crowd, cackling to one another occasionally, in a subdued tone; but the instant we appeared again, their necks came out like telescopes, and setting up a great noise, which meant, I have no doubt, 'What, you would go, would you! What do you think of it! How do you like it!' they attended us to the outer gate, and cast us forth, derisively, into Mantua.

The geese who saved the Capitol,[19] were, as compared to these, pork to the learned pig. What a gallery it was! I would take their opinion on a question of art, in preference to the discourses of Sir Joshua Reynolds.

Now that we were standing in the street, after being thus ignominiously escorted thither, my little friend was plainly reduced to the 'píccolo gíro', or little circuit of the town, he had formerly proposed. But my suggestion that we should visit the Palazzo Tè (of which I had heard a great deal, as a strange wild place) imparted new life to him, and away we went.

The secret of the length of Midas's ears, would have been more extensively known, if that servant of his, who whispered it to the reeds, had lived in Mantua, where there are reeds and rushes enough to have published it to all the world. The Palazzo Tè stands in a swamp, among this sort of vegetation; and is, indeed, as singular a place as I ever saw.

Not for its dreariness, though it is very dreary. Not for its dampness, though it is very damp. Nor for its desolate condition, though it is as desolate and neglected as house can be. But chiefly for the unaccountable nightmares with which its interior has been decorated (among other subjects of more delicate execution) by Giulio Romano. There is a leering giant over a certain chimney piece, and there are dozens of giants (Titans warring with Jove) on the walls of another room, so inconceivably ugly and grotesque, that it is marvellous how any man can have imagined such creatures. In the chamber in which they abound, these monsters, with swollen faces and cracked cheeks, and every kind of distortion of look and limb, are depicted as staggering under the weight of falling buildings, and being overwhelmed in the ruins; upheaving masses of rock, and burying themselves beneath; vainly striving to sustain the pillars of heavy roofs that topple down upon their heads; and, in a word, undergoing and doing every kind of mad and demoniacal destruction. The figures are immensely large, and exaggerated to the utmost pitch of uncouthness; the colouring is harsh and disagreeable; and the whole effect more like (I should imagine) a violent rush of blood to the head of the spectator, than any real picture set before him by the hand of an artist. This apoplectic performance was shown by a sickly looking woman, whose appearance was referable, I dare say, to the bad air of the marshes; but it was difficult to help feeling as if she were too much haunted by the giants, and they were frightening her to death, all alone in that exhausted cistern of a palace, among the reeds and rushes, with the mists hovering about outside, and stalking round and round it continually.

Our walk through Mantua showed us, in almost every street, some suppressed church: now used for a warehouse, now for nothing at all: all as crazy and dismantled as they could be, short of tumbling down bodily. The marshy town was so intensely dull and flat, that the dirt upon it seemed not to have come there in the ordinary course, but to have settled and mantled on its surface as on standing water. And yet there were some business dealings going on, and some profits realising; for there were arcades full of Jews, where those extraordinary people were sitting outside their shops, contemplating their stores of stuffs, and woollens, and bright handkerchiefs, and trinkets: and looking, in all respects, as wary and business-like, as their brethren in Houndsditch, London.

Having selected a Vetturíno from among the neighbouring Christians, who agreed to carry us to Milan in two days and a half, and to start, next morning, as soon as the gates were opened, I returned to the Golden Lion, and dined luxuriously in my own room, in a narrow passage between two bedsteads, confronted by a smoky fire, and backed up by a chest of drawers. At six o'clock next morning, we were jingling in the dark through the wet cold mist that enshrouded the town; and, before noon, the driver (a native of Mantua, and sixty years of age or thereabouts) began *to ask the way* to Milan.

It lay through Bozzolo – formerly a little republic, and now one of the most deserted and poverty-stricken of towns – where the landlord of the miserable inn (God bless him! it was his weekly custom) was distributing infinitesimal coins among a clamorous herd of women and children, whose rags were fluttering in the wind and rain outside his door, where they were gathered to receive his charity. It lay through mist, and mud, and rain, and vines trained low upon the ground, all that day and the next; the first sleeping-place being Cremona, memorable for its dark brick churches, and immensely high tower, the Torrazzo – to say nothing of its violins, of which it certainly produces none in these degenerate days; and the second, Lodi. Then we went on, through more mud, mist, and rain, and marshy ground: and through such a fog, as Englishmen, strong in the faith of their own grievances, are apt to believe is nowhere to be found but in their own country, until we entered the paved streets of Milan.

The fog was so dense here, that the spire of the far-famed cathedral might as well have been at Bombay, for anything that could be seen of it at that time. But as we halted to refresh, for a few days then, and returned to Milan again next summer, I had ample opportunities of seeing the glorious structure in all its majesty and beauty.

All Christian homage to the saint who lies within it! There are many good and true saints in the calendar, but San Carlo Borromeo has – if I may quote Mrs. Primrose[20] on such a subject – 'my warm heart'. A charitable doctor to the sick, a munificent friend to the poor, and this, not in any spirit of blind bigotry, but as the bold opponent of enormous abuses in the Romish church, I honour his memory. I honour it none the less, because he was nearly slain by a priest, suborned, by priests, to murder him at the altar, in acknowledgment of his endeavours to reform a false and hypocritical brotherhood of monks. Heaven shield all imitators of San Carlo Borromeo as it shielded him! A reforming Pope would need a little shielding, even now.

The subterranean chapel in which the body of San Carlo Borromeo is preserved, presents as striking and as ghastly a contrast, perhaps, as any place can show. The tapers which are lighted down there, flash and gleam on alti-rilievi in gold and silver, delicately wrought by skilful hands, and representing the principal events in the life of the saint. Jewels, and precious metals, shine and sparkle on every side. A windlass slowly removes the front of the altar; and, within it, in a gorgeous shrine of gold and silver, is seen, through alabaster, the shrivelled mummy of a man, the pontifical robes with which it is adorned, radiant with diamonds, emeralds, rubies, every costly and magnificent gem. The shrunken heap of poor earth in the midst of this great glitter, is more pitiful than if it lay upon a dunghill. There is not a ray of imprisoned light in all the flash and fire of jewels, but seems to mock the dusty holes where eyes were, once. Every thread of silk in the rich vestments seems only a provision from the worms that spin, for the behoof of worms that propagate in sepulchres.

In the old refectory of the dilapidated Convent of Santa Maria delle Grazie, is the work of art, perhaps, better known than any other in the world: *The Last Supper*, by Leonardo da Vinci – with a door cut through it by the intelligent Dominican friars, to facilitate their operations at dinnertime.

I am not mechanically acquainted with the art of painting, and have no other means of judging of a picture than as I see it resembling and refining upon nature, and presenting graceful combinations of forms and colours. I am, therefore, no authority whatever, in reference to the 'touch' of this or that master; though I know very well (as anybody may, who chooses to think about the matter) that few very great masters can possibly have painted, in the compass of their lives, one half of the pictures that bear their names, and that are recognised by many aspirants to a reputation for taste, as undoubted originals. But this, by the way. Of *The Last Supper*, I would simply observe, that in its beautiful composition and arrangement, there it is, at Milan, a wonderful picture; and that, in its original colouring, or in its original expression of any single face or feature, there it is not. Apart from the damage it has sustained from damp, decay, or neglect, it has been (as Barry shows)[21] so retouched upon, and repainted, and that so clumsily, that many of the heads are, now, positive deformities, with patches of paint and plaster sticking upon them like wens, and utterly distorting the expression. Where the original artist set that impress of his genius on a face, which, almost in a line or touch, separated him from meaner painters and made him what he was, succeeding bunglers, filling up, or painting across seams and cracks, have been quite unable to imitate his hand; and putting in some scowls, or frowns, or wrinkles, of their own, have blotched and spoiled the work. This is so well established as an historical fact, that I should not repeat it, at the risk of being tedious, but for having observed an English gentleman before the picture, who was at great pains to fall into what I may describe as mild convulsions, at certain minute details of expression which are not left in it. Whereas, it would be comfortable and rational for travellers and critics to arrive at a general understanding that it cannot fail to have been a work of extraordinary merit once, when, with so few of its original beauties remaining, the grandeur of the general design is yet sufficient to sustain it, as a piece replete with interest and dignity.

We achieved the other sights of Milan, in due course, and a fine city it is, though not so unmistakably Italian as to possess the characteristic qualities of many towns far less important in themselves. The Corso, where the Milanese gentry ride up and down in carriages, and rather than not do which, they would half starve themselves at home, is a most noble public promenade, shaded by long avenues of trees. In the splendid theatre of La Scala, there was a ballet of action performed after the opera, under the title of *Prometheus*: in the beginning of which, some hundred or two of men and women represented our mortal race before the refinements of the arts and sciences, and loves and graces, came on earth to soften them. I never saw anything more effective. Generally speaking, the pantomimic action of the Italians is more remarkable for its sudden and impetuous character than for its delicate expression; but, in this case, the drooping monotony, the weary, miserable, listless, moping life, the sordid passions and desires of human creatures, destitute of those elevating influences to which we owe so much, and to whose promoters we render so little, were expressed in a manner really powerful and affecting. I should have thought it almost impossible to present such an idea so strongly on the stage, without the aid of speech.

Milan soon lay behind us, at five o'clock in the morning; and before the golden statue on the summit of the cathedral spire was lost in the blue sky, the Alps, stupendously confused in lofty peaks and ridges, clouds and snow, were towering in our path.

Still, we continued to advance toward them until nightfall; and, all day long, the mountain tops presented strangely shifting shapes, as the road displayed them in different points of view. The beautiful day was just declining, when we came upon the Lago Maggiore, with its lovely islands. For however fanciful and fantastic the Isola Bella may be, and is, it still is beautiful. Anything springing out of that blue water, with that scenery around it, must be.

It was ten o'clock at night when we got to Domo d'Ossola, at the foot of the Pass of the Simplon. But as the moon was shining brightly, and there was not a cloud in the starlit sky, it was no time for going to bed, or going anywhere but on. So, we got a little carriage, after some delay, and began the ascent.

It was late in November; and the snow lying four or five feet thick in the beaten road on the summit (in other parts the new drift was already deep), the air was piercing cold. But, the serenity of the night, and the grandeur of the road, with its impenetrable shadows, and deep glooms, and its sudden turns into the shining of the moon and its incessant roar of falling water, rendered the journey more and more sublime at every step.

Soon leaving the calm Italian villages below us, sleeping in the moonlight, the road began to wind among dark trees, and after a time emerged upon a barer region, very steep and toilsome, where the moon shone bright and high. By degrees, the roar of water grew louder; and the stupendous track, after crossing the torrent by a bridge, struck in between two massive perpendicular walls of rock that quite shut out the moonlight, and only left a few stars shining in the narrow strip of sky above. Then, even this was lost, in the thick darkness of a cavern in the rock, through which the way was pierced; the terrible cataract thundering and roaring close below it, and its foam and spray hanging, in a mist, about the entrance. Emerging from this cave, and coming again into the moonlight, and across a dizzy bridge, it crept and twisted upward, through the Gorge of Gondo, savage and grand beyond description, with smooth-fronted precipices, rising up on either hand, and almost meeting overhead. Thus we went, climbing on our rugged way, higher and higher all night, without a moment's weariness, lost in the contemplation of the black rocks, the tremendous heights and depths, the fields of smooth snow lying, in the clefts and hollows, and the fierce torrents thundering headlong down the deep abyss.

Towards daybreak, we came among the snow, where a keen wind was blowing fiercely. Having, with some trouble, awakened the inmates of a wooden house in this solitude, round which the wind was howling dismally, catching up the snow in wreaths and hurling it away, we got some breakfast in a room built of rough timbers, but well warmed by a stove, and well contrived (as it had need to be) for keeping out the bitter storms. A sledge being then made ready, and four horses harnessed to it, we went, ploughing, through the snow. Still upward, but now in the cold light of morning, and with the great white desert on which we travelled, plain and clear.

We were well upon the summit of the mountain, and had before us the rude cross of wood, denoting its greatest altitude above the sea, when the light of the rising sun, struck, all at once, upon the waste of snow, and turned it a deep red. The lonely grandeur of the scene was then at its height.

As we went sledging on, there came out of the hospice founded by Napoleon, a group of peasant travellers, with staves and knapsacks, who had rested there last night: attended by a monk or two, their hospitable entertainers, trudging slowly forward with them, for company's sake. It was pleasant to give them good morning, and pretty, looking back a long way after them, to see them looking back at us, and hesitating presently, when one of our horses stumbled and fell, whether or no they should return and help us. But he was soon up again, with the assistance of a rough wagoner whose team had stuck fast there too; and when we had helped him out of his difficulty, in return, we left him slowly ploughing towards them, and went slowly and swiftly forward, on the brink of a steep precipice, among the mountain pines.

Taking to our wheels again, soon afterwards, we began rapidly to descend; passing under everlasting glaciers, by means of arched galleries, hung with clusters of dripping icicles; under and over foaming waterfalls; near places of refuge, and galleries of shelter against sudden danger; through caverns over whose arched roofs the avalanches slide, in spring, and bury themselves in the unknown gulf beneath. Down, over lofty bridges, and through horrible ravines, a little shifting speck in the vast desolation of ice and snow, and monstrous granite rocks; down through the deep Gorge of the Saltine, and deafened by the torrent plunging madly down, among the riven blocks of rock, into the level country, far below. Gradually down, by zigzag roads, lying between an upward and a downward precipice, into warmer weather, calmer air, and softer scenery, until there lay before us, glittering like gold or silver in the thaw and sunshine, the metal-covered, red, green, yellow, domes and church spires of a Swiss town.

The business of these recollections being with Italy, and my business, consequently, being to scamper back thither as fast as possible, I will not recall (though I am sorely tempted) how the Swiss villages, clustered at the feet of giant mountains, looked like playthings; or how confusedly the houses were heaped and piled together; or how there were very narrow streets to shut the howling winds out in the winter time; and broken bridges, which the impetuous torrents, suddenly released in spring, had swept away. Or how there were peasant women here, with great round fur caps, looking, when they peeped out of casements and only their heads were seen, like a population of sword bearers to the Lord Mayor of London; or how the town of Vevey, lying on the smooth lake of Geneva, was beautiful to see; or how the statue of Saint Peter in the street at Fribourg, grasps the largest key that ever was beheld; or how Fribourg is illustrious for its two suspension bridges, and its grand cathedral organ.

Or how, between that town and Bâle, the road meandered among thriving villages of wooden cottages, with overhanging thatched roofs, and low protruding windows, glazed with small round panes of glass like crown-pieces; or how, in every little Swiss homestead, with its cart or wagon carefully stowed away beside the house, its little garden, stock of poultry, and groups of red-cheeked children, there was an air of comfort, very new and very pleasant after Italy; or how the dresses of the women changed again, and there were no more sword bearers to be seen; and fair white stomachers, and great black, fan-shaped, gauzy-looking caps, prevailed instead.

Or how the country by the Jura mountains, sprinkled with snow, and lighted by the moon, and musical with falling water, was delightful; or how, below the windows of the great hotel of the Three Kings at Bâle, the swollen Rhine ran fast and green; or how, at Strasbourg, it was quite as fast but not as green, and was said to be foggy lower down, and, at that late time of the year, was a far less certain means of progress, than the highway road to Paris.

Or how Strasbourg itself, in its magnificent old Gothic Cathedral, and its ancient houses with their peaked roofs and gables, made a little gallery of quaint and interesting views; or how a crowd was gathered inside the cathedral at noon, to see the famous mechanical clock in motion, striking twelve. How, when it struck twelve, a whole army of puppets went through many ingenious evolutions; and, among them, a huge puppet-cock, perched on the top, crowed twelve times, loud and clear. Or how it was wonderful to see this cock at great pains to clap its wings, and strain its throat; but obviously having no connection whatever with its own voice; which was deep within the clock, a long way down.

Or how the road to Paris, was one sea of mud, and thence to the coast, a little better for a hard frost. Or how the cliffs of Dover were a pleasant sight, and England was so wonderfully neat though dark, and lacking colour on a winter's day, it must be conceded.

Or how, a few days afterwards, it was cool, recrossing the channel, with ice upon the decks, and snow lying pretty deep in France. Or how the Malle Poste scrambled through the snow, headlong, drawn in the hilly parts by any number of stout horses at a canter; or how there were, outside the post office yard in Paris, before daybreak, extraordinary adventurers in heaps of rags, groping in the snowy streets with little rakes, in search of odds and ends.

Or how, between Paris and Marseilles, the snow being then exceeding deep, a thaw came on, and the mail waded rather than rolled for the next three hundred miles or so; breaking springs on Sunday nights, and putting out its two passengers to warm and refresh themselves pending the repairs, in miserable billiard rooms, where hairy company, collected about stoves, were playing cards; the cards being very like themselves – extremely limp and dirty.

Or how there was detention at Marseilles from stress of weather; and steamers were advertised to go, which did not go; or how the good steam packet *Charlemagne* at length put out, and met such weather that now she threatened to run into Toulon, and now into Nice, but, the wind moderating, did neither, but ran on into Genoa harbour instead, where the familiar bells rang sweetly in my ear. Or how there was a travelling party on board, of whom one member was very ill in the cabin next to mine, and being ill was cross, and therefore declined to give up the dictionary, which he kept under his pillow; thereby obliging his companions to come down to him, constantly, to ask what was the Italian for a lump of sugar, a glass of brandy-and-water, what's o'clock? and so forth: which he always insisted on looking out, with his own seasick eyes, declining to entrust the book to any man alive.

Like Grumio, I might have told you, in detail, all this and something more – but to as little purpose – were I not deterred by the remembrance that my business is with Italy. Therefore, like Grumio's story, it 'shall die in oblivion'.[22]

A Flight

When Don Diego de – I forget his name – the inventor of the last new flying machines, price so many francs for ladies, so many more for gentlemen – when Don Diego, by permission of Deputy Chaff Wax and his noble band,[23] shall have taken out a patent for the Queen's dominions, and shall have opened a commodious warehouse in an airy situation; and when all persons of any gentility will keep at least a pair of wings, and be seen skimming about in every direction; I shall take a flight to Paris (as I soar round the world) in a cheap and independent manner. At present, my reliance is on the South Eastern Railway Company, in whose express train here I sit, at eight of the clock on a very hot morning, under the very hot roof of the terminus at London Bridge, in danger of being 'forced' like a cucumber or a melon, or a pineapple – and talking of pineapples, I suppose there never were so many pineapples in a train as there appear to be in this train.

Whew! The hothouse air is faint with pineapples. Every French citizen or citizeness is carrying pineapples home. The compact little enchantress in the corner of my carriage (French actress, to whom I yielded up my heart under the auspices of that brave child, 'Meat-chell,' at the St. James's Theatre the night before last[24]) has a pineapple in her lap. Compact Enchantress's friend, confidante, mother, mystery, Heaven knows what, has two pineapples in her lap, and a bundle of them under the seat. Tobacco-smoky Frenchman in Algerine wrapper, with peaked hood behind, who might be Abd-el-Kader dyed rifle-green,[25] and who seems to be dressed entirely in dirt and braid, carries pineapples in a covered basket. Tall, grave, melancholy Frenchman, with black Vandyke beard, and hair close-cropped, with expansive chest to waistcoat, and compressive waist to coat, saturnine as to his pantaloons, calm as to his feminine boots, precious as to his jewellery, smooth and white as to his linen, dark-eyed, high-foreheaded, hawk-nosed – got up, one thinks, like Lucifer or Mephistopheles, or Zamiel, transformed into a highly genteel Parisian – has the green end of a pineapple sticking out of his neat valise.

Whew! If I were to be kept here long, under this forcing-frame, I wonder what would become of me – whether I should be forced into a giant, or should sprout or blow into some other phenomenon! Compact Enchantress is not ruffled by the heat – she is always composed, always compact. O look at her little ribbons, frills, and edges, at her shawl, at her gloves, at her hair, at her bracelets, at her bonnet, at everything about her! How is it accomplished? What does she do to be so neat? How is it that every trifle she wears belongs to her, and cannot choose but be a part of her? And even Mystery, look at *her*! A model. Mystery is not young, not pretty, though still of an average candlelight passability; but she does such miracles in her own behalf, that, one of these days, when she dies, they'll be amazed to find an old woman in her bed, distantly like her. She was an actress once, I shouldn't wonder, and had a Mystery attendant on herself. Perhaps, Compact Enchantress will live to be a Mystery, and to wait with a shawl at the side-scenes, and to sit opposite to mademoiselle in railway carriages, and smile and talk subserviently, as Mystery does now. That's hard to believe!

Two Englishmen, and now our carriage is full. First Englishman, in the monied interest – flushed – highly respectable – Stock Exchange, perhaps – City, certainly. Faculties of second Englishman entirely absorbed in hurry. Plunges into the carriage, blind. Calls out of window concerning his luggage, deaf. Suffocates himself under pillows of greatcoats, for no reason, and in a demented manner. Will receive no assurance from any porter whatsoever. Is stout and hot, and wipes his head, and makes himself hotter by breathing so hard. Is totally incredulous respecting assurance of Collected Guard, that 'there's no hurry'. No hurry! And a flight to Paris in eleven hours!

It is all one to me in this drowsy corner, hurry or no hurry. Until Don Diego shall send home my wings, my flight is with the South-Eastern Company. I can fly with the South-Eastern, more lazily, at all events, than in the upper air. I have but to sit here thinking as idly as I please, and be whisked away. I am not accountable to anybody for the idleness of my thoughts in such an idle summer flight; my flight is provided for by the South-Eastern and is no business of mine.

The bell! With all my heart. It does not require *me* to do so much as even to flap my wings. Something snorts for me, something shrieks for me, something proclaims to everything else that it had better keep out of my way – and away I go.

Ah! The fresh air is pleasant after the forcing-frame, though it does blow over these interminable streets, and scatter the smoke of this vast wilderness of chimneys. Here we are – no, I mean there we were, for it has darted far into the rear – in Bermondsey where the tanners live. Flash! The distant shipping in the Thames is gone. Whirr! The little streets of new brick and red tile, with here and there a flagstaff growing like a tall weed out of the scarlet beans, and, everywhere, plenty of open sewer and ditch for the promotion of the public health, have been fired off in a volley. Whizz! Dust heaps, market gardens, and waste rounds. Rattle! New Cross Station. Shock! There we were at Croydon. Bur-r-r! The tunnel.

I wonder why it is that when I shut my eyes in a tunnel I begin to feel as if I were going at an express pace the other way. I am clearly going back to London now. Compact Enchantress must have forgotten something, and reversed the engine. No! After long darkness, pale fitful streaks of light appear. I am still flying on for Folkestone. The streaks grow stronger – become continuous – become the ghost of day – become the living day – became I mean – the tunnel is miles and miles away, and here I fly through sunlight, all among the harvest and the Kentish hops.

There is a dreamy pleasure in this flying. I wonder where it was, and when it was, that we exploded, blew into space somehow, a parliamentary train, with a crowd of heads and faces looking at us out of cages, and some hats waving. Monied Interest says it was at Reigate Station. Expounds to Mystery how Reigate Station is so many miles from London, which Mystery again develops to Compact Enchantress. There might be neither a Reigate nor a London for me, as I fly away among the Kentish hops and harvest. What do *I* care?

Bang! We have let another station off, and fly away regardless. Everything is flying. The hop gardens turn gracefully towards me, presenting regular avenues of hops in rapid flight, then whirl away. So do the pools and rushes, haystacks, sheep, clover in full bloom delicious to the sight and smell, corn sheaves, cherry orchards, apple orchards, reapers, gleaners, hedges, gates, fields that taper off into little angular corners, cottages, gardens, now and then a church. Bang, bang! A double-barrelled station! Now a wood, now a bridge, now a landscape, now a cutting, now a – Bang! a single-barrelled station – there was a cricket match somewhere with two white tents, and then four flying cows, then turnips – now the wires of the electric telegraph are all alive, and spin, and blur their edges, and go up and down, and make the intervals between each other most irregular, contracting and expanding in the strangest manner. Now we slacken. With a screwing, and a grinding, and a smell of water thrown on ashes, now we stop!

Demented Traveller, who has been for two or three minutes watchful, clutches his greatcoats, plunges at the door, rattles it, cries 'Hi!' eager to embark on board of impossible packets, far inland. Collected Guard appears.

'Are you for Tunbridge, sir?'

'Tunbridge? No. Paris.'

'Plenty of time, sir. No hurry. Five minutes here, sir, for refreshment.'

I am so blest (anticipating Zamiel, by half a second) as to procure a glass of water for Compact Enchantress.

Who would suppose we had been flying at such a rate, and shall take wing again directly? Refreshment room full, platform full, porter with watering pot deliberately cooling a hot wheel, another porter with equal deliberation helping the rest of the wheels bountifully to ice cream. Monied Interest and I re-entering the carriage first, and being there alone, he intimates to me that the French are 'no go' as a nation. I ask why? He says, that Reign of Terror of theirs was quite enough. I ventured to inquire whether he remembers anything that preceded said Reign of Terror? He says not particularly. 'Because,' I remark, 'the harvest that is reaped, has sometimes been sown.' Monied Interest repeats, as quite enough for him, that the French are revolutionary, 'and always at it'.

Bell. Compact Enchantress, helped in by Zamiel (whom the stars confound!), gives us her charming little side-box look, and smites me to the core. Mystery eating sponge cake, pineapple atmosphere faintly tinged with suspicions of sherry. Demented Traveller flits past the carriage, looking for it. Is blind with agitation, and can't see it. Seems singled out by destiny to be the only unhappy creature in the flight, who has any cause to hurry himself. Is nearly left behind. Is seized by Collected Guard after the Train is in motion, and bundled in. Still, has lingering suspicions that there must be a boat in the neighbourhood, and *will* look wildly out of window for it.

Flight resumed. Corn sheaves, hop gardens, reapers, gleaners, apple orchards, cherry orchards, stations single- and double-barrelled, Ashford. Compact Enchantress (constantly talking to Mystery, in an exquisite manner) gives a little scream; a sound that seems to come from high up in her precious little head; from behind her bright little eyebrows. 'Great Heaven, my pineapple! My angel! It is lost!' Mystery is desolated. A search made. It is not lost. Zamiel finds it. I curse him (flying) in the Persian manner. May his face be turned upside down, and jackasses sit upon his uncle's grave!

Now fresher air, now glimpses of unenclosed down-land with flapping crows flying over it whom we soon out-fly, now the sea, now Folkestone at a quarter after ten. 'Tickets ready, gentlemen!' Demented dashes at the door. 'For Paris, sir? No hurry.'

Not the least. We are dropped slowly down to the port, and sidle to and fro (the whole Train) before the insensible Royal George Hotel, for some ten minutes. The Royal George takes no more heed of us than its namesake under water at Spithead, or under earth at Windsor, does.[26] The Royal George's dog lies winking and blinking at us, without taking the trouble to sit up; and the Royal George's 'wedding party' at the open window (who seem, I must say, rather tired of bliss) don't bestow a solitary glance upon us, flying thus to Paris in eleven hours. The first gentleman in Folkestone is evidently used up, on this subject.

Meanwhile, Demented chafes. Conceives that every man's hand is against him, and exerting itself to prevent his getting to Paris. Refuses consolation. Rattles door. Sees smoke on the horizon, and 'knows' it's the boat gone without him. Monied Interest resentfully explains that *he* is going to Paris too. Demented signifies, that if Monied Interest chooses to be left behind, *he* don't.

'Refreshments in the waiting room, ladies and gentlemen. No hurry, ladies and gentlemen, for Paris. No hurry whatever!'

Twenty minutes' pause, by Folkestone clock, for looking at Enchantress while she eats a sandwich, and at Mystery while she eats of everything there that is eatable, from porkpie, sausage, jam, and gooseberries, to lumps of sugar. All this time, there is a very waterfall of luggage, with a spray of dust, tumbling slantwise from the pier into the steamboat. All this time, Demented (who has no business with it) watches it with starting eyes, fiercely requiring to be shown *his* luggage. When it at last concludes the cataract, he rushes hotly to refresh – is shouted after, pursued, jostled, brought back, pitched into the departing steamer upside down, and caught by mariners disgracefully.

A lovely harvest day, a cloudless sky, a tranquil sea. The piston rods of the engines so regularly coming up from below, to look (as well they may) at the bright weather, and so regularly almost knocking their iron heads against the cross beam of the skylight, and never doing it! Another Parisian actress is on board, attended by another Mystery. Compact Enchantress greets her sister artist – Oh, the Compact One's pretty teeth! – and Mystery greets Mystery. *My* Mystery soon ceases to be conversational – is taken poorly, in a word, having lunched too miscellaneously – and goes below. The remaining Mystery then smiles upon the sister artists (who, I am afraid, wouldn't greatly mind stabbing each other), and is upon the whole ravished.

And now I find that all the French people on board begin to grow, and all the English people to shrink. The French are nearing home, and shaking off a disadvantage, whereas we are shaking it on. Zamiel is the same man, and Abd-el-Kader is the same man, but each seems to come into possession of an indescribable confidence that departs from us – from Monied Interest, for instance, and from me. Just what they gain, we lose. Certain British 'Gents' about the steersman, intellectually nurtured at home on parody of everything and truth of nothing, become subdued, and in a manner forlorn; and when the steersman tells them (not unexultingly) how he has 'been upon this station now eight year, and never see the old town of Bullun yet', one of them, with an imbecile reliance on a reed, asks him what he considers to be the best hotel in Paris?

Now, I tread upon French ground, and am greeted by the three charming words, Liberty, Equality, Fraternity, painted up (in letters a little too thin for their height) on the custom house wall – also by the sight of large cocked hats, without which demonstrative headgear nothing of a public nature can be done upon this soil. All the rabid hotel population of Boulogne howl and shriek outside a distant barrier, frantic to get at us. Demented, by some unlucky means peculiar to himself, is delivered over to their fury, and is presently seen struggling in a whirlpool of touters – is somehow understood to be going to Paris – is, with infinite noise, rescued by two cocked hats, and brought into custom house bondage with the rest of us.

Here, I resign the active duties of life to an eager being, of preternatural sharpness, with a shelving forehead and a shabby snuff-coloured coat, who (from the wharf) brought me down with his eye before the boat came into port. He darts upon my luggage, on the floor where all the luggage is strewn like a wreck at the bottom of the great deep; gets it proclaimed and weighed as the property of 'Monsieur a traveller unknown'; pays certain francs for it, to a certain functionary behind a pigeon hole, like a pay-box at a theatre (the arrangements in general are on a wholesale scale, half-military and half-theatrical); and I suppose I shall find it when I come to Paris – he says I shall. I know nothing about it, except that I pay him his small fee, and pocket the ticket he gives me, and sit upon a counter, involved in the general distraction.

Railway station. 'Lunch or dinner, ladies and gentlemen. Plenty of time for Paris. Plenty of time!' Large hall, long counter, long strips of dining table, bottles of wine, plates of meat, roast chickens, little loaves of bread, basins of soup, little carafes of brandy, cakes, and fruit. Comfortably restored from these resources, I begin to fly again.

I saw Zamiel (before I took wing) presented to Compact Enchantress and Sister Artist, by an officer in uniform, with a waist like a wasp's, and pantaloons like two balloons. They all got into the next carriage together, accompanied by the two Mysteries. They laughed. I am alone in the carriage (for I don't consider Demented anybody) and alone in the world.

Fields, windmills, low grounds, pollard trees, windmills, fields, fortifications, Abbeville, soldiering and drumming. I wonder where England is, and when I was there last – about two years ago, I should say. Flying in and out among these trenches and batteries, skimming the clattering drawbridges, looking down into the stagnant ditches, I become a prisoner of state, escaping. I am confined with a comrade in a fortress. Our room is in an upper story. We have tried to get up the chimney, but there's an iron grating across it, imbedded in the masonry. After months of labour, we have worked the grating loose with the poker, and can lift it up. We have also made a hook, and twisted our rugs and blankets into ropes. Our plan is, to go up the chimney, hook our ropes to the top, descend hand over hand upon the roof of the guardhouse far below, shake the hook loose, watch the opportunity of the sentinels pacing away, hook again, drop into the ditch, swim across it, creep into the shelter of the wood. The time is come – a wild and stormy night. We are up the chimney, we are on the guardhouse roof, we are swimming in the murky ditch, when lo! 'Qui v'la?' A bugle, the alarm, a crash! What is it? Death? No, Amiens.

More fortifications, more soldiering and drumming, more basins of soup, more little loaves of bread, more bottles of wine, more carafes of brandy, more time for refreshment. Everything good, and everything ready. Bright, unsubstantial-looking, scenic sort of station. People waiting. Houses, uniforms, beards, moustaches, some sabots, plenty of neat women, and a few old-visaged children. Unless it be a delusion born of my giddy flight, the grown-up people and the children seem to change places in France. In general, the boys and girls are little old men and women, and the men and women lively boys and girls.

Bugle, shriek, flight resumed. Monied Interest has come into my carriage. Says the manner of refreshing is 'not bad', but considers it French. Admits great dexterity and politeness in the attendants. Thinks a decimal currency may have something to do with their despatch in settling accounts, and don't know but what it's sensible and convenient. Adds, however, as a general protest, that they're a revolutionary people – and always at it.

Ramparts, canals, cathedral, river, soldiering and drumming, open country, river, earthenware manufactures, Creil. Again ten minutes. Not even Demented in a hurry. Station, a drawing room with a veranda: like a planter's house. Monied Interest considers it a bandbox, and not made to last. Little round tables in it, at one of which the Sister Artists and attendant Mysteries are established with Wasp and Zamiel, as if they were going to stay a week.

Anon, with no more trouble than before, I am flying again, and lazily wondering as I fly. What has the South-Eastern done with all the horrible little villages we used to pass through, in the *Diligence*? What have they done with all the summer dust, with all the winter mud, with all the dreary avenues of little trees, with all the ramshackle postyards, with all the beggars (who used to turn out at night with bits of lighted candle, to look in at the coach windows), with all the long-tailed horses who were always biting one another, with all the big postilions in jack-boots – with all the mouldy cafés that we used to stop at, where a long mildewed tablecloth, set forth with jovial bottles of vinegar and oil, and with a Siamese arrangement of pepper and salt, was never wanting? Where are the grass-grown little towns, the wonderful little marketplaces all unconscious of markets, the shops that nobody kept, the streets that nobody trod, the churches that nobody went to, the bells that nobody rang, the tumbledown old buildings plastered with many-coloured bills that nobody read? Where are the two-and-twenty weary hours of long, long day and night journey, sure to be either insupportably hot or insupportably cold? Where are the pains in my bones, where are the fidgets in my legs, where is the Frenchman with the nightcap who never *would* have the little coupé window down, and who always fell upon me when he went to sleep, and always slept all night snoring onions?

A voice breaks in with 'Paris! Here we are!'

I have overflown myself, perhaps, but I can't believe it. I feel as if I were enchanted or bewitched. It is barely eight o'clock yet – it is nothing like half-past – when I have had my luggage examined at that briskest of custom houses attached to the station, and am rattling over the pavement in a hackney cabriolet.

Surely, not the pavement of Paris? Yes, I think it is, too. I don't know any other place where there are all these high houses, all these haggard-looking wine shops, all these billiard tables, all these stocking makers with flat red or yellow legs of wood for signboard, all these fuel shops with stacks of billets painted outside, and real billets sawing in the gutter, all these dirty corners of streets, all these cabinet pictures over dark doorways representing discreet matrons nursing babies. And yet this morning – I'll think of it in a warm bath.

Very like a small room that I remember in the Chinese Baths upon the boulevard, certainly; and, though I see it through the steam, I think that I might swear to that peculiar hot-linen basket, like a large wicker hourglass. When can it have been that I left home? When was it that I paid 'through to Paris' at London Bridge, and discharged myself of all responsibility, except the preservation of a voucher ruled into three divisions, of which the first was snipped off at Folkestone, the second aboard the boat, and the third taken at my journey's end? It seems to have been ages ago. Calculation is useless. I will go out for a walk.

The crowds in the streets, the lights in the shops and balconies, the elegance, variety, and beauty of their decorations, the number of the theatres, the brilliant cafes with their windows thrown up high and their vivacious groups at little tables on the pavement, the light and glitter of the houses turned as it were inside out, soon convince me that it is no dream; that I am in Paris, howsoever I got there. I stroll down to the sparkling Palais Royal, up the Rue de Rivoli, to the Place Vendôme. As I glance into a print-shop window, Monied Interest, my late travelling companion, comes upon me, laughing with the highest relish of disdain.

'Here's a people!' he says, pointing to Napoleon in the window and Napoleon on the column. 'Only one idea all over Paris! A monomania!'

Humph! I *think* I have seen Napoleon's match? There *was* a statue, when I came away, at Hyde Park Corner, and another in the City, and a print or two in the shops.

I walk up to the Barrière de l'Etoile, sufficiently dazed by my flight to have a pleasant doubt of the reality of everything about me; of the lively crowd, the overhanging trees, the performing dogs, the hobby horses, the beautiful perspectives of shining lamps, the hundred and one enclosures, where the singing is, in gleaming orchestras of azure and gold, and where a star-eyed Houri comes round with a box for voluntary offerings. So, I pass to my hotel, enchanted; sup, enchanted; go to bed, enchanted; pushing back this morning (if it really were this morning) into the remoteness of time, blessing the South-Eastern Company for realising the Arabian Nights in these prose days, murmuring, as I wing my idle flight into the land of dreams, 'No hurry, ladies and gentlemen, going to Paris in eleven hours. It is so well done, that there really is no hurry!'

The Calais Night Mail

It is an unsettled question with me whether I shall leave Calais something handsome in my will, or whether I shall leave it my malediction. I hate it so much, and yet I am always so very glad to see it, that I am in a state of constant indecision on this subject.

When I first made acquaintance with Calais, it was as a maundering young wretch in a clammy perspiration and dripping saline particles, who was conscious of no extremities but the one great extremity, seasickness – who was a mere bilious torso, with a mislaid headache somewhere in its stomach – who had been put into a horrible swing in Dover harbour, and had tumbled giddily out of it on the French coast, or the Isle of Man, or anywhere. Times have changed, and now I enter Calais self-reliant and rational. I know where it is beforehand, I keep a look out for it, I recognise its landmarks when I see any of them, I am acquainted with its ways, and I know – and I can bear – its worst behaviour.

Malignant Calais! Low-lying alligator, evading the eyesight and discouraging hope! Dodging flat streak, now on this bow, now on that, now anywhere, now everywhere, now nowhere! In vain Cape Grinez, coming frankly forth into the sea, exhorts the failing to be stout of heart and stomach: sneaking Calais, prone behind its bar, invites emetically to despair. Even when it can no longer quite conceal itself in its muddy dock, it has an evil way of falling off, has Calais, which is more hopeless than its invisibility. The pier is all but on the bowsprit and you think you are there – roll, roar, wash! – Calais has retired miles inland, and Dover has burst out to look for it. It has a last dip and slide in its character, has Calais, to be especially commanded to the infernal gods. Thrice accursed be that garrison town, when it dives under the boat's keel, and comes up a league or two to the right, with the packet shivering and spluttering and staring about for it!

Not but what I have my animosities towards Dover. I particularly detest Dover for the self-complacency with which it goes to bed. It always goes to bed (when I am going to Calais) with a more brilliant display of lamp and candle than any other town. Mr and Mrs Birmingham, host and hostess of the Lord Warden Hotel, are my much-esteemed friends, but they are too conceited about the comforts of that establishment when the night mail is starting. I know it is a good house to stay at, and I don't want the fact insisted upon in all its warm bright windows at such an hour. I know the Warden is a stationary edifice that never rolls or pitches, and I object to its big outline seeming to insist upon that circumstance, and, as it were, to come over me with it, when I am reeling on the deck of the boat. Beshrew the Warden likewise, for obstructing that corner, and making the wind so angry as it rushes round. Shall I not know that it blows quite soon enough, without the officious Warden's interference?

As I wait here on board the night packet, for the South-Eastern train to come down with the mail, Dover appears to me to be illuminated for some intensely aggravating festivity in my personal dishonour. All its noises smack of taunting praises of the land, and dispraises of the gloomy sea, and of me for going on it. The drums upon the heights have gone to bed, or I know they would rattle taunts against me for having my unsteady footing on this slippery deck. The many gas eyes of the Marine Parade twinkle in an offensive manner, as if with derision. The distant dogs of Dover bark at me in my misshapen wrappers, as if I were Richard the Third.[27]

A screech, a bell, and two red eyes come gliding down the Admiralty Pier with a smoothness of motion rendered more smooth by the heaving of the boat. The sea makes noises against the pier, as if several hippopotami were lapping at it, and were prevented by circumstances over which they had no control from drinking peaceably. We, the boat, become violently agitated – rumble, hum, scream, roar, and establish an immense family washing day at each paddle-box. Bright patches break out in the train as the doors of the post office vans are opened, and instantly stooping figures with sacks upon their backs begin to be beheld among the piles, descending as it would seem in ghostly procession to Davy Jones's locker. The passengers come on board; a few shadowy Frenchmen, with hatboxes shaped like the stoppers of gigantic case-bottles; a few shadowy Germans in immense fur coats and boots; a few shadowy Englishmen prepared for the worst and pretending not to expect it. I cannot disguise from my uncommercial mind the miserable fact that we are a body of outcasts; that the attendants on us are as scant in number as may serve to get rid of us with the least possible delay; that there are no night-loungers interested in us; that the unwilling lamps shiver and shudder at us; that the sole object is to commit us to the deep and abandon us. Lo, the two red eyes glaring in increasing distance, and then the very train itself has gone to bed before we are off!

What is the moral support derived by some sea-going amateurs from an umbrella? Why do certain voyagers across the Channel always put up that article, and hold it up with a grim and fierce tenacity? A fellow creature near me – whom I only know to *be* a fellow creature, because of his umbrella: without which he might be a dark bit of cliff, pier, or bulkhead – clutches that instrument with a desperate grasp, that will not relax until he lands at Calais. Is there any analogy, in certain constitutions, between keeping an umbrella up, and keeping the spirits up? A hawser thrown on board with a flop replies

'Stand by!'
'Stand by, below!'
'Half a turn a head!'
'Half a turn a head!'
'Half speed!'
'Half speed!'
'Port!'

'Port!'

'Steady!'

'Steady!'

'Go on!'

'Go on!'

A stout wooden wedge driven in at my right temple and out at my left, a floating deposit of lukewarm oil in my throat, and a compression of the bridge of my nose in a blunt pair of pincers, – these are the personal sensations by which I know we are off, and by which I shall continue to know it until I am on the soil of France. My symptoms have scarcely established themselves comfortably, when two or three skating shadows that have been trying to walk or stand, get flung together, and another two or three shadows in tarpaulin slide with them into corners and cover them up. Then the South Foreland lights begin to hiccup at us in a way that bodes no good.

It is at about this period that my detestation of Calais knows no bounds. Inwardly I resolve afresh that I never will forgive that hated town. I have done so before, many times, but that is past. Let me register a vow. Implacable animosity to Calais everm– that was an awkward sea, and the funnel seems of my opinion, for it gives a complaining roar.

The wind blows stiffly from the Nor-East, the sea runs high, we ship a deal of water, the night is dark and cold, and the shapeless passengers lie about in melancholy bundles, as if they were sorted out for the laundress; but for my own uncommercial part I cannot pretend that I am much inconvenienced by any of these things. A general howling whistling flopping gurgling and scooping, I am aware of, and a general knocking about of Nature; but the impressions I receive are very vague. In a sweet faint temper, something like the smell of damaged oranges, I think I should feel languidly benevolent if I had time. I have not time, because I am under a curious compulsion to occupy myself with the Irish melodies. 'Rich and rare were the gems she wore' is the particular melody to which I find myself devoted.[28] I sing it to myself in the most charming manner and with the greatest expression. Now and then, I raise my head (I am sitting on the hardest of wet seats, in the most uncomfortable of wet attitudes, but I don't mind it) and notice that I am a whirling shuttlecock between a fiery battledore of a lighthouse on the French coast and a fiery battledore of a lighthouse on the English coast; but I don't notice it particularly, except to feel envenomed in my hatred of Calais. Then I go on again, 'Rich and rare were the ge-ems she-e-e-e wore, And a bright gold ring on her wa-and she bo-ore, But O her beauty was fa-a-a-a-r beyond' – I am particularly proud of my execution here, when I become aware of another awkward shock from the sea, and another protest from the funnel, and a fellow creature at the paddle-box more audibly indisposed than I think he need be – 'Her sparkling gems, or snow-white wand, But O her beauty was fa-a-a-a-r beyond' – another awkward one here, and the fellow creature with the umbrella down and picked up – 'Her spa-a-rkling ge-ems, or her' Port! port! steady! steady! snow-white fellow creature at the paddle-box very selfishly audible, bump, roar, wash, 'white wand.'

As my execution of the Irish melodies partakes of my imperfect perceptions of what is going on around me, so what is going on around me becomes something else than what it is. The stokers open the furnace doors below, to feed the fires, and I am again on the box of the old Exeter Telegraph fast coach, and that is the light of the forever extinguished coach lamps, and the gleam on the hatches and paddle-boxes is *their* gleam on cottages and haystacks, and the monotonous noise of the engines is the steady jingle of the splendid team. Anon, the intermittent funnel roar of protest at every violent roll, becomes the regular blast of a high pressure engine, and I recognise the exceedingly explosive steamer in which I ascended the Mississippi when the American civil war was not, and when only its causes were. A fragment of mast on which the light of a lantern falls, an end of rope, and a jerking block or so, become suggestive of Franconi's circus at Paris where I shall be this very night mayhap (for it must be morning now), and they dance to the selfsame time and tune as the trained steed, Black Raven. What may be the speciality of these waves as they come rushing on, I cannot desert the pressing demands made upon me by the gems she wore, to inquire, but they are charged with something about Robinson Crusoe, and I think it was in Yarmouth Roads that he first went a seafaring and was near foundering (what a terrific sound that word had for me when I was a boy!) in his first gale of wind. Still, through all this, I must ask her (who *was* she I wonder!) for the fiftieth time, and without ever stopping, Does she not fear to stray, So lone and lovely through this bleak way, And are Erin's sons so good or so cold, As not to be tempted by more fellow creatures at the paddle-box or gold? Sir Knight I feel not the least alarm, No son of Erin will offer me harm, For though they love fellow creature with umbrella down again and golden store, Sir Knight they what a tremendous one love honour and virtue more: For though they love Stewards with a bull's eye bright, they'll trouble you for your ticket, sir – rough passage tonight!

I freely admit it to be a miserable piece of human weakness and inconsistency, but I no sooner become conscious of those last words from the steward than I begin to soften towards Calais. Whereas I have been vindictively wishing that those Calais burghers who came out of their town by a short cut into the History of England, with those fatal ropes round their necks by which they have since been towed into so many cartoons, had all been hanged on the spot, I now begin to regard them as highly respectable and virtuous tradesmen. Looking about me, I see the light of Cape Grinez well astern of the boat on the davits to leeward, and the light of Calais harbour undeniably at its old tricks, but still ahead and shining. Sentiments of forgiveness of Calais, not to say of attachment to Calais, begin to expand my bosom. I have weak notions that I will stay there a day or two on my way back. A faded and recumbent stranger pausing in a profound reverie over the rim of a basin, asks me what kind of place Calais is? I tell him (Heaven forgive me!) a very agreeable place indeed – rather hilly than otherwise.

So strangely goes the time, and on the whole so quickly – though still I seem to have been on board a week – that I am bumped rolled gurgled washed and pitched into Calais Harbour before her maiden smile has finally lighted her through the Green Isle, When blest for ever is she who relied, On entering Calais at the top of the tide. For we have not to land tonight down among those slimy timbers – covered with green hair as if it were the mermaids' favourite combing-place – where one crawls to the surface of the jetty, like a stranded shrimp, but we go steaming up the harbour to the Railway Station Quay. And as we go, the sea washes in and out among piles and planks, with dead heavy beats and in quite a furious manner (whereof we are proud), and the lamps shake in the wind, and the bells of Calais striking one seem to send their vibrations struggling against troubled air, as we have come struggling against troubled water. And now, in the sudden relief and wiping of faces, everybody on board seems to have had a prodigious double-tooth out, and to be this very instant free of the dentist's hands. And now we all know for the first time how wet and cold we are, and how salty we are; and now I love Calais with my heart of hearts!

'Hôtel Dessin!' (but in this one case it is not a vocal cry; it is but a bright lustre in the eyes of the cheery representative of that best of inns.)

'Hôtel Meurice!'

'Hôtel de France!'

'Hôtel de Calais!'

'The Royal Hôtel, Sir, Angaishe ouse!'

'You going to Parry, Sir?'

'Your baggage, registair froo, Sir?'

Bless ye, my touters, bless ye, my commissionaires, bless ye, my hungry-eyed mysteries in caps of a military form, who are always here, day or night, fair weather or foul, seeking in-scrutable jobs which I never see you get! Bless ye, my custom-house officers in green and grey; permit me to grasp the welcome hands that descend into my travelling-bag, one on each side, and meet at the bottom to give my change of linen a peculiar shake up, as if it were a measure of chaff or grain! I have nothing to declare, Monsieur le Douanier, except that when I cease to breathe, Calais will be found written on my heart. No article liable to local duty have I with me, Monsieur l'Officier de l'Octroi, unless the overflowing of a breast devoted to your charming town should be in that wise chargeable. Ah! see at the gangway by the twinkling lantern, my dearest brother and friend, he once of the Passport Office, he who collects the names! May he be for ever changeless in his buttoned black surtout, with his notebook in his hand, and his tall black hat, surmounting his round smiling patient face! Let us embrace, my dearest brother. I am yours *à tout jamais* – for the whole of ever.

Calais up and doing at the railway station, and Calais down and dreaming in its bed; Calais with something of 'an ancient and fish-like smell'[29] about it, and Calais blown and sea-washed pure; Calais represented at the buffet by savoury roast fowls, hot coffee, cognac, and Bordeaux; and Calais represented everywhere by flitting persons with a monomania for changing money – though I never shall be able to understand in my present state of existence how they live by it, but I suppose I should, if I understood the currency question – Calais *en gros*, and Calais *en détail*, forgive one who has deeply wronged you – I was not fully aware of it on the other side, but I meant Dover.

Ding, ding! To the carriages, gentlemen the travellers. Ascend then, gentlemen the travellers, for Hazebroucke, Lille, Douai, Bruxelles, Arras, Amiens, and Paris! I, humble rep-resentative of the uncommercial interest, ascend with the rest. The train is light tonight, and I share my compartment with but two fellow-travellers; one, a compatriot in an obsolete cravat, who thinks it a quite unaccountable thing that they don't keep 'London time' on a French railway, and who is made angry by my modestly suggesting the possibility of Paris time being more in their way; the other, a young priest, with a very small bird in a very small cage, who feeds the small bird with a quill, and then puts him up in the network above his head, where he advances twittering, to his front wires, and seems to address me in an electioneering manner. The compatriot (who crossed in the boat, and whom I judge to be some person of distinction, as he was shut up, like a stately species of rabbit, in a private hutch on deck) and the young priest (who joined us at Calais) are soon asleep, and then the bird and I have it all to ourselves.

A stormy night still; a night that sweeps the wires of the electric telegraph with a wild and fitful hand; a night so very stormy, with the added storm of the train progress through it, that when the guard comes clambering round to mark the tickets while we are at full speed (a really horrible performance in an express train, though he holds on to the open window by his elbows in the most deliberate manner), he stands in such a whirlwind that I grip him fast by the collar, and feel it next to manslaughter to let him go. Still, when he is gone, the small, small bird remains at his front wires feebly twittering to me – twittering and twittering, until, leaning back in my place and looking at him in drowsy fascination, I find that he seems to jog my memory as we rush along.

Uncommercial travels (thus the small, small bird) have lain in their idle thriftless way through all this range of swamp and dyke, as through many other odd places; and about here, as you very well know, are the queer old stone farmhouses, approached by drawbridges, and the windmills that you get at by boats. Here, are the lands where the women hoe and dig, paddling canoe-wise from field to field, and here are the cabarets and other peasant houses where the stone dovecotes in the littered yards are as strong as warders' towers in old castles. Here, are the long monotonous miles of canal, with the great Dutch-built barges garishly painted, and the towing girls, sometimes harnessed by the forehead, sometimes by the girdle and the shoulders, not a pleasant sight to see. Scattered through this country are mighty works of Vauban, whom you know about, and regiments of such corporals as you heard of once upon a time, and many a blue-eyed Bebelle.[30] Through these flat districts, in the shining summer days, walk those long, grotesque files of young novices in enormous shovel hats, whom you remember blackening the ground chequered by the avenues of leafy trees. And now that Hazebroucke slumbers certain kilometres ahead, recall the summer evening when your dusty feet strolling up from the station tended haphazard to a fair there, where the oldest inhabitants were circling round and round a barrel-organ on hobby horses, with the greatest gravity, and where the principal show in the fair was a Religious Richardson's[31] – literally, on its own announcement in great letters, 'THEATRE RELIGIEUX'. In which improving temple, the dramatic representation was of 'all the interesting events in the life of our Lord, from the Manger to the Tomb'; the principal female character, without any reservation or exception, being at the moment of your arrival, engaged in trimming the external moderators (as it was growing dusk), while the next principal female character took the money, and the young St John disported himself upside down on the platform.

Looking up at this point to confirm the small, small bird in every particular he has mentioned, I find he has ceased to twitter, and has put his head under his wing. Therefore, in my different way I follow the good example.

Some Account of an Extraordinary Traveller

No longer ago than this Easter time last past, we became acquainted with the subject of the present notice. Our knowledge of him is not by any means an intimate one, and is only of a public nature. We have never interchanged any conversation with him, except on one occasion when he asked us to have the goodness to take off our hat, to which we replied, 'Certainly.'

Mr Booley was born (we believe) in Rood Lane, in the City of London. He is now a gentleman advanced in life, and has for some years resided in the neighbourhood of Islington. His father was a wholesale grocer (perhaps), and he was (possibly) in the same way of business; or he may, at an early age, have become a clerk in the Bank of England, or in a private bank, or in the India House. It will be observed that we make no pretence of having any information in reference to the private history of this remarkable man, and that our account of it must be received as rather speculative than authentic.

In person Mr Booley is below the middle size, and corpulent. His countenance is florid, he is perfectly bald, and soon hot; and there is a composure in his gait and manner, calculated to impress a stranger with the idea of his being, on the whole, an unwieldy man. It is only in his eye that the adventurous character of Mr Booley is seen to shine. It is a moist, bright eye, of a cheerful expression, and indicative of keen and eager curiosity.

It was not until late in life that Mr Booley conceived the idea of entering on the extraordinary amount of travel he has since accomplished. He had attained the age of sixty-five before he left England for the first time. In all the immense journeys he has since performed, he has never laid aside the English dress, nor departed in the slightest degree from English customs. Neither does he speak a word of any language but his own.

Mr Booley's powers of endurance are wonderful. All climates are alike to him. Nothing exhausts him; no alternations of heat and cold appear to have the least effect upon his hardy frame. His capacity of travelling, day and night, for thousands of miles, has never been approached by any traveller of whom we have any knowledge through the help of books. An intelligent Englishman may have occasionally pointed out to him objects and scenes of interest; but otherwise he has travelled alone and unattended. Though remarkable for personal cleanliness, he has carried no luggage; and his diet has been of the simplest kind. He has often found a biscuit, or a bun, sufficient for his support over a vast tract of country. Frequently, he has travelled hundreds of miles, fasting, without the least abatement of his natural spirits. It says much for the Total Abstinence cause, that Mr Booley has never had recourse to the artificial stimulus of alcohol, to sustain him under his fatigues.

His first departure from the sedentary and monotonous life he had hitherto led, strikingly exemplifies, we think, the energetic character, long suppressed by that unchanging routine. Without any communication with any member of his family – Mr Booley has never been married, but has many relations – without announcing his intention to his solicitor, or banker, or any person entrusted with the management of his affairs, he closed the door of his house behind him at one o'clock in the afternoon of a certain day, and immediately proceeded to New Orleans, in the United States of America.

His intention was to ascend the Mississippi and Missouri rivers, to the base of the Rocky Mountains. Taking his passage in a steamboat without loss of time, he was soon upon the bosom of the Father of Waters, as the Indians call the mighty stream which, night and day, is always carrying huge instalments of the vast continent of the New World, down into the sea.

Mr Booley found it singularly interesting to observe the various stages of civilisation obtaining on the banks of these mighty rivers. Leaving the luxury and brightness of New

Orleans – a somewhat feverish luxury and brightness, he observed, as if the swampy soil were too much enriched in the hot sun with the bodies of dead slaves – and passing various towns in every stage of progress, it was very curious to observe the changes of civilisation and of vegetation too. Here, while the doomed Negro race were working in the plantations, while the republican overseer looked on, whip in hand, tropical trees were growing, beautiful flowers in bloom; the alligator, with his horribly sly face, and his jaws like two great saws, was basking on the mud; and the strange moss of the country was hanging in wreaths and garlands on the trees, like votive offerings. A little farther towards the west, and the trees and flowers were changed, the moss was gone, younger infant towns were rising, forests were slowly disappearing, and the trees, obliged to aid in the destruction of their kind, fed the heavily breathing monster that came clanking up those solitudes laden with the pioneers of the advancing human army. The river itself, that moving highway, showed him every kind of floating contrivance, from the lumbering flat-bottomed boat, and the raft of logs, upward to the steamboat, and downward to the poor Indian's frail canoe. A winding thread through the enormous range of country, unrolling itself before the wanderer like the magic skein in the story, he saw it tracked by wanderers of every kind, roaming from the more settled world, to those first nests of men. The floating theatre, dwelling-house, hotel, museum, shop; the floating mechanism for screwing the trunks of mighty trees out of the mud, like antediluvian teeth; the rapidly flowing river, mid the blazing woods; he left them all behind – town, city, and log cabin, too; and floated up into the prairies and savannahs, among the deserted lodges of tribes of savages, and among their dead, lying alone on little wooden stages with their stark faces upward towards the sky. Among the blazing grass, and herds of buffaloes and wild horses, and among the wigwams of the fast-declining Indians, he began to consider how, in the eternal current of progress setting across this globe in one unchangeable direction, like the unseen agency that points the needle to the pole, the chiefs who only dance the dances of their fathers, and will never have a new figure for a new tune, and the me-dicine-men who know no medicine but what was medicine a hundred years ago, must be surely and inevitably swept from the earth, whether they be Choctawas, Maudans, Britons, Austrians, or Chinese.

He was struck, too, by the reflection that savage nature was not by any means such a fine and noble spectacle as some delight to represent it. He found it a poor, greasy, paint-plastered, miserable thing enough; but a very little way above the beasts in most respects; in many customs a long way below them. It occurred to him that the 'Big Bird', or the 'Blue Fish', or any of the other braves, was but a troublesome braggart after all; making a mighty whooping and halloaing about nothing particular, doing very little for science, not much more than the monkeys for art, scarcely anything worth mentioning for letters, and not often making the world greatly better than he found it. Civilisation, Mr Booley concluded, was, on the whole, with all its blemishes, a more imposing sight, and a far better thing to stand by.

Mr Booley's observations of the celestial bodies, on this voyage, were principally confined to the discovery of the alarming fact that light had altogether departed from the moon; which presented the appearance of a white dinner plate. The clouds, too, conducted themselves in an extraordinary manner, and assumed the most eccentric forms, while the sun rose and set in a very reckless way. On his return to his native country, however, he had the satisfaction of finding all these things as usual.

It might have been expected that at his advanced age, retired from the active duties of life, blest with a competency, and happy in the affections of his numerous relations, Mr Booley would now have settled himself down, to muse, for the remainder of his days, over the new stock of experience thus acquired.

But travel had whetted, not satisfied, his appetite; and remembering that he had not seen the Ohio River, except at the point of its junction with the Mississippi, he returned to the United States, after a short interval of repose, and appearing suddenly at Cincinnati, the queen City of the West, traversed the clear waters of the Ohio to its Falls. In this expedition he had the pleasure of encountering a party of intelligent workmen from Birmingham who were making the same tour. Also his nephew Septimus, aged only thirteen. This intrepid boy had started from Peckham, in the old country, with two and sixpence sterling in his pocket; and had, when he encountered his uncle at a point of the Ohio River, called Snaggy Bar, still one shilling of that sum remaining!

Again at home, Mr Booley was so pressed by his appetite for knowledge as to remain at home only one day. At the expiration of that short period, he actually started for New Zealand.

It is almost incredible that a man in Mr Booley's station of life, however adventurous his nature, and however few his artificial wants, should cast himself on a voyage of thirteen thousand miles from Great Britain with no other outfit than his watch and purse, and no arms but his walking stick. We are, however, assured on the best authority, that thus he made the passage out, and thus appeared, in the act of wiping his smoking head with his pocket handkerchief, at the entrance to Port Nicholson in Cook's Straits: with the very spot within his range of vision, where his illustrious predecessor, Captain Cook, so unhappily slain at Otaheite, once anchored.

After contemplating the swarms of cattle maintained on the hills in this neighbourhood, and always to be found by the stockmen when they are wanted, though nobody takes any care of them – which Mr Booley considered the more remarkable, as their natural objection to being killed might be supposed to be augmented by the beauty of the climate – Mr Booley proceeded to the town of Wellington. Having minutely examined it in every point, and made himself perfect master of the whole natural history and process of manufacture of the flax plant, with its splendid yellow blossoms, he repaired to a Native Pa, which, unlike the Native Pa to which he was accustomed, he found to be a town, and not a parent. Here he observed a chief with a long spear, making every demonstration of spitting a visitor, but really giving him the Maori or welcome – a word Mr Booley is inclined to derive from the known hospitality of our English mayors – and here also he observed some Europeans rubbing noses, by way of shaking hands, with the aboriginal inhabitants. After participating in an affray between the natives and the English soldiers, in which the former were defeated with great loss, he plunged into the bush, and there camped out for some months, until he had made a survey of the whole country.

While leading this wild life, encamped by night near a stream for the convenience of water, in a ware, or lint, built open in the front, with a roof sloping backward to the ground, and made of poles, covered and enclosed with bark or fern, it was Mr Booley's singular fortune to encounter Miss Creeble, of The Misses Creeble's Boarding and Day Establishment for Young Ladies, Kennington Oval, who, accompanied by three of her young ladies in search of information, had achieved this marvellous journey, and was then also in the bush. Miss Creeble, having very unsettled opinions on the subject of gunpowder, was afraid that it entered into the composition of the fire before the tent, and that something would presently blow up or go off. Mr Booley, as a more experienced traveller, assuring her that there was no danger; and calming the fears of the young ladies, an acquaintance commenced between them. They accomplished the rest of their travels in New Zealand together, and the best understanding prevailed among the little party. They took notice of the trees, as the Kaikatea, the Kauri, the Ruta, the Pukatea, the Hinau, and the Tanakaka – names which Miss Creeble had a bland relish in pronouncing. They admired the beautiful, arborescent, palm-like fern, abounding everywhere, and frequently exceeding thirty feet in height. They wondered at the curious owl, who is supposed to demanded, 'More Pork!' wherever he flies,[32] and whom Miss Creeble termed, 'an admonition of Nature's against greediness!' And they contemplated some very rampant natives, of cannibal propensities. After many pleasing and instructive vicissitudes, they returned to England in company, where the ladies were safely put into a hackney cabriolet by Mr Booley, in Leicester Square, London.

And now, indeed, it might have been imagined that that roving spirit, tired of rambling about the world, would have settled down at home in peace and honour. Not so. After repairing to the tubular bridge across the Menai Straits, and accompanying Her Majesty on her visit to Ireland (which he characterised as 'a magnificent exhibition'), Mr Booley, with his usual absence of preparation, departed for Australia.

Here again, he lived out in the bush, passing his time chiefly among the working-gangs of convicts who were carrying timber. He was much impressed by the ferocious mastiffs chained to barrels, who assist the sentries in keeping guard over those misdoers. But he observed that the atmosphere in this part of the world, unlike the descriptions he had read of it, was extremely thick, and that objects were misty, and difficult to be discerned. From a certain unsteadiness and trembling, too, which he frequently remarked on the face of nature, he was led to conclude that this part of the globe was subject to convulsive heavings and earthquakes. This caused him to return with some precipitation.

Again at home, and probably reflecting that the countries he had hitherto visited were new in the history of man, this extraordinary traveller resolved to proceed up the Nile to the second cataract. At the next performance of the great ceremony of 'opening the Nile', at Cairo, Mr Booley was present.

Along that wonderful river, associated with such stupendous fables, and with a history more prodigious than any fancy of man, in its vast and gorgeous facts; among temples, palaces, pyramids, colossal statues, crocodiles, tombs, obelisks, mummies, sand and ruin; he proceeded, like an opium eater in a mighty dream. Thebes rose before him. An avenue of two hundred sphinxes, with not a head among them, – one of six or eight, or ten such avenues, all leading to a common centre – conducted to the Temple of Carnak: its walls, eighty feet high and twenty-five feet thick, a mile and three-quarters in circumference; the interior of its tremendous hall, occupying an area of forty-seven thousand square feet, large enough to hold four great Christian churches, and yet not more than one-seventh part of the entire ruin. Obelisks he saw, thousands of years of age, as sharp as if the chisel had cut their edges yesterday; colossal statues fifty-two feet high, with 'little' fingers five feet and a half long; a very world of ruins, that were marvellous old ruins in the days of Herodotus; tombs cut high up in the rock, where European travellers live solitary, as in stony crow's nests, burning mummied Thebans, gentle and simple – of the dried blood-royal maybe – for their daily fuel, and making articles of furniture of their dusty coffins. Upon the walls of temples, in colours fresh and bright as those of yesterday, he read the conquests of great Egyptian monarchs; upon the tombs of humbler people in the same blooming symbols, he saw their ancient way of working at their trades, of riding, driving, feasting, playing games; of marrying and burying, and performing on instruments, and singing songs, and healing by the power of animal magnetism, and performing all the occupations of life. He visited the quarries of Silsileh, whence nearly all the red stone used by the ancient Egyptian architects and sculptors came; and there beheld enormous singled-stoned colossal figures, nearly finished – redly snowed up, as it were, and trying hard to break out – waiting for the finishing touches, never to be given by the mummied hands of thousands of years ago. In front of the temple of Abou Simbel, he saw gigantic figures sixty feet in height and twenty one across the shoulders, dwarfing live men on camels down to pigmies. Elsewhere he beheld complacent monsters tumbled down like ill-used dolls of a titanic make, and staring with stupid benignity at the arid earth whereon their huge faces rested. His last look of that amazing land was at the Great Sphinx, buried in the sand – sand in its eyes, sand in its ears, sand drifted on its broken nose, sand lodging, feet deep, in the ledges of its head – struggling out of a wide sea of sand, as if to look hopelessly forth for the ancient glories once surrounding it.

In this expedition, Mr Booley acquired some curious information in reference to the language of hieroglyphics. He encountered the simoon in the desert, and lay down, with the rest of his caravan until it had passed over. He also beheld on the horizon some of those stalking pillars of sand, apparently reaching from earth to heaven, which, with the red sun shining through them, so terrified the Arabs attendant on Bruce, that they fell prostrate, crying that the Day of Judgment was come.[33] More Copts, Turks, Arabs, Fellahs, Bedouins, Mosques, Mamelukes, and Moosulmen he saw, than we have space to tell. His days were all Arabian Nights, and he saw wonders without end.

This might have satiated any ordinary man, for a time at least. But Mr Booley, being no ordinary man, within twenty-four hours of his arrival at home was making the overland journey to India.

He has emphatically described this as 'a beautiful piece of scenery' and 'a perfect picture'. The appearance of Malta and Gibraltar he can never sufficiently commend. In crossing the desert from Grand Cairo to Suez, he was particularly struck by the undulations of the sandscape (he preferred that word to landscape, as more expressive of the region), and by the incident of beholding a caravan upon its line of march; a spectacle which in the remembrance always affords him the utmost pleasure. Of the stations on the desert, and the cinnamon gardens of Ceylon, he likewise entertains a lively recollection. Calcutta he praises also; though he has been heard to observe that the British military at that seat of government were not as well proportioned as he could desire the soldiers of his country to be; and that the breed of horses there in use was susceptible of some improvement.

Once more in his native land, with the vigour of his constitution unimpaired by the many toils and fatigues he had encountered, what had Mr Booley now to do, but, full of years and honour, to recline upon the grateful appreciation of his Queen and country, always eager to distinguish peaceful merit? What had he now to do, but to receive the decoration ever ready to be bestowed, in England, on men deservedly distinguished, and to take his place among the best? He had this to do. He had yet to achieve the most astonishing enterprise for which he was reserved. In all the countries he had yet visited, he had seen no frost and snow. He resolved to make a voyage to the ice-bound Arctic Regions.

In pursuance of this surprising determination, Mr Booley accompanied the expedition under Sir James Ross, consisting of Her Majesty's ships the *Enterprise* and *Investigator*, which sailed from the river Thames on the 12th May 1848, and which, on the 11th September, entered Port Leopold Harbour.

In this inhospitable region, surrounded by eternal ice, cheered by no glimpse of the sun, shrouded in gloom and darkness, Mr Booley passed the entire winter. The ships were covered in, and fortified all round with walls of ice and snow; the masts were frozen up; hoar frost settled on the yards, tops, shrouds, stays, and rigging; around, in every direction, lay an interminable waste, on which only the bright stars, the yellow moon, and the vivid Aurora Borealis looked, by night or day.

And yet the desolate sublimity of this astounding spectacle was broken in a pleasant and surprising manner. In the remote solitude to which he had penetrated, Mr Booley (who saw no Eskimos during his stay, though he looked for them in every direction) had the happiness of encountering two Scotch gardeners; several English compositors, accompanied by their wives; three brass founders from the neighbourhood of Long Acre, London; two coach painters, a gold beater and his only daughter, by trade a staymaker; and several other working people from sundry parts of Great Britain who had conceived the extraordinary idea of 'holidaymaking' in the frozen wilderness. Hither, too, had Miss Creeble and her three young ladies penetrated; the latter attired in braided peacoats of a comparatively light material; and Miss Creeble defended from the inclemency of a polar winter by no other outer garment than a wadded polka-jacket. He found this courageous lady in the act of explaining, to the youthful sharers of her toils, the various phases of nature by which they were surrounded. Her explanations were principally wrong, but her intentions always admirable.

Cheered by the society of these fellow adventurers, Mr Booley slowly glided on into the summer season. And now, at midnight, all was bright and shining. Mountains of ice, wedged and broken into the strangest forms – jagged points, spires, pinnacles, pyramids, turrets, columns in endless succession and in infinite variety, flashing and sparkling with ten thousand hues, as though the treasures of the earth were frozen up in all that water – appeared on every side. Masses of ice, floating and driving hither and thither, menaced the hardy voyagers with destruction; and threatened to crush their strong ships, like nutshells. But, below those ships was clear seawater, now; the fortifying walls were gone; the yards, tops, shrouds and rigging, free from that hoary rust of long inaction, showed like themselves again; and the sails, bursting from the masts, like foliage which the welcome sun at length developed, spread themselves to the wind, and wafted the travellers away.

In the short interval that has elapsed since his safe return to the land of his birth, Mr Booley has decided on no new expedition; but he feels that he will yet be called upon to undertake one, perhaps of greater magnitude than any he has achieved, and frequently remarks, in his own easy way, that he wonders where the deuce he will he taken to next! Possessed of good health and good spirits, with powers unimpaired by all he has gone through, mixed with an increase of appetite still growing with what it feeds on, what may not be expected yet from this extraordinary man!

It was only at the close of Easter week that, sitting in an armchair, at a private club called the Social Oysters, assembling at Highbury Barn, where he is much respected, this indefatigable traveller expressed himself in the following terms,

'It is very gratifying to me,' said he, 'to have seen so much at my time of life, and to have acquired a knowledge of the countries I have visited, which I could not have derived from books alone. When I was a boy, such travelling would have been impossible, as the gigantic-moving-panorama or diorama mode of conveyance, which I have principally adopted (all my modes of conveyance have been pictorial), had then not been attempted. It is a delightful characteristic of these times, that new and cheap means are continually being devised for conveying the results of actual experience to those who are unable to obtain such experiences for themselves: and to bring them within the reach of the people – emphatically of the people; for it is they at large who are addressed in these endeavours, and not exclusive audiences. Hence,' said Mr Booley, 'even if I see a run on an idea, like the panorama one, it awakens no illhumour within me, but gives me pleasant thoughts. Some of the best results of actual travel are suggested by such means to those whose lot it is to stay at home. New worlds open out to them, beyond their little worlds, and widen their range of reflection, information, sympathy, and interest. The more man knows of man, the better for the common brotherhood among us all. I shall, therefore,' said Mr Booley, 'now propose to the Social Oysters, the healths of Mr Banvard, Mr Brees, Mr Phillips, Mr Allen, Mr Prout, Messrs Bonomi, Fahey, and Warren, Mr Thomas Grieve, and Mr Burford.[34] Long life to them all, and more power to their pencils!'

The Social Oysters having drunk this toast with acclamation, Mr Booley proceeded to entertain them with anecdotes of his travels. This he is in the habit of doing after they have feasted together, according to the manner of Sinbad the Sailor – except that he does not bestow upon the Social Oysters the munificent reward of one hundred sequins per night, for listening.

Notes

1. A 'black border of artificial workmanship' would suggest a black eye.
2. The wheel was a form of punishment. Some would be productive, being a tread wheel to produce corn for example, whilst others had no function other than punishment through forced labour.
3. Historians researching the Roman satirist Gaius Lucilius encountered some confusion surrounding his date of birth, which according to various sources could be anytime between 180 and 148 BC.
4. In the fairy tale, Fatima was the last wife of Bluebeard (he had seven in total), whose curiosity led to the discovery that he had murdered his last six wives.
5. An 'absentee' is Dickens' euphemism for a convict sent out to Australia.
6. In Dickens' *Barnaby Rudge*, written over the course of 1841, the landlord John Willet sees his inn destroyed by rioters. His reaction is a shocked stupor that freezes him completely, 'awake as to his eyes, certainly, but with all his powers of reason and reflection in a sound and dreamless sleep', fwatching the events unfold 'as if it were some queer play or entertainment, of an astonishing, and stupefying nature, but having no reference to himself'.
7. Dickens introduces the lazy gentleman in the opening chapter of *American Notes*. The gentleman tells everyone how he has made the transatlantic trip thirteen times already, and is keen to show, as a seasoned traveller, how unextraordinary it all is to him: 'inquiring with a yawn if another gentleman whether he is "going across" – as if it were a ferry.'
8. A mustard poultice comprised of mustard seed made into a paste and applied to a bandage in order to provide heat to the applied body area, thus increasing perspiration and circulation.
9. An extinguisher: a pump and hose on ship for use in fires.
10. Thomas Potter Cooke was a nineteenth-century English actor who frequently played a sailor.
11. Italian coach drivers.
12. *Romeo and Juliet*, Act One Scene Five: 'O, she doth teach the torches to burn bright!'
13. The tomb of ill-fated Juliet.
14. In Laurence Sterne's *Tristram Shandy*, the parson Yorick is supposed to find consolation, after his death, 'to hear his monumental inscription read over with such a variety of plaintive tones' by numerous visitors to his grave.
15. *Romeo and Juliet*, Act One, Scene One.
16. *Romeo and Juliet*, Act Three, Scene Three.
17. Romeo describes the apothecary as 'poor... bare and full of wretchedness... Famine is in thy cheeks,/Need and Oppression starveth

in thy eyes,/Contempt and beggary hangs upon thy back.' Act Five, Scene Three.

18. The Brave Courier, Louis Roche, was a companion to the Dickens family throughout their travels in Italy, organising accommodation and suchlike. Dickens noted how the courier, 'best of servants and most beaming of men', was assumed by others to be the head of the party both as a consequence of the care he took organising everything for them, and in his more impressive physical stature than the young Dickens.

19. In Roman History, the city was alerted to the approach of invading Gauls when geese started honking loudly in alarm.

20. A character from Oliver Goldsmith's *The Vicar of Wakefield*.

21. James Barry was an English painter under the patronage of Edmund Burke who went abroad from 1765 to 1771. His letters to the Burkes include various commentaries on continental art.

22. From *The Taming of the Shrew*, Act Four, Scene One, where Petruchio's servant Grumio, complaining that his fellow servant Curtis keeps interrupting him, cuts his story short proclaiming that it 'now shall die of oblivion and thou return inexperienced to thy grave'. Like Dickens, the irony is that before announcing this, Grumio summarises all the key points of his story; both he and Dickens tell their tale under assumed protest of not being allowed to tell it.

23. The Chaff-Wax, one of the Lord Chancellor's officers, fitted the sealing wax for patents and other documents.

24. 'Meat-chell' is John Mitchell, who presented various French plays during the 1840s and 1850s at St James' Theatre in London.

25. Abd-el-Kader was the Amir of Mascara who led a fifteen year campaign against the French during their occupation of Algeria. After taking an oath to cause no more uprisings in Algeria, in 1860 he repressed an outbreak in Damascus, saving many Christians and, ironically, becoming a French hero, after which he was awarded the Legion of Honour and toured Paris and London.

26. The first Royal George is a celebated naval ship that sank in 1782 in Spithead, just off the coast of the Isle of Wight. he second Royal George is King George III, buried at Windsor in 1820.

27. In Shakespeare's *Richard III* the protagonist claims he is made up 'so lamely and unfashionably/That dogs bark at me as I halt by them.' Act One Scene One.

28. 'Rich and rare were the gems she wore', is a ballad written by Thomas Moore in 1807 as part of his collection entitled *Irish Melodies*.

29. From *The Tempest*, Act Two, Scene Two, where Trinculo, investigating the hidden Caliban, declares him to be 'A fish: he smells like a fish, a very ancient and fish-like smell.'

30. Bebelle, 'a playful name for Gabrielle', is a character from Dickens' short story 'His Boots' from *Somebody's Luggage*. Like many children in Dickens' writings, she is innocent, pure and disadvantaged.

31. John Richardson was an early nineteenth-century showman, whose name became synonymous with portable theatres. The religious variations on portable theatres incorporated stories from the Bible.

32. The Ruru, a small owl indigenous to New Zealand, is also known colloquially as the Morepork because of its distinctive cry, prompting Dickens' pun.

33. James Bruce was a Scottish explorer who travelled across Africa in the eighteenth century, trying to discover the source of the Nile. During a trek across the desert in 1772, the party were blighted by simoons, presumably the incident to which Dickens refers here.

34. These men were all artists, creators of panoramas.

Biographical note

Charles Dickens (1812–70), a true celebrity in the Victorian period, remains one of the most well-known British writers. His most popular works, such as *Great Expectations* (1861) and *A Christmas Carol* (1843), continue to be read and adapted worldwide. In addition to fourteen complete novels, Dickens wrote short stories, essays, and plays.

Dickens' early life was financially and emotionally unstable, and when his father was imprisoned for debt, he was sent to work in a blacking factory, an experience which haunted his later fiction. Dickens worked as an office-boy and court reporter before his *Sketches by Boz* (1836–7) brought his writing to the attention of the publishing house Chapman and Hall. After the success of *The Posthumous Papers of the Pickwick Club*, Dickens was able to found the journal *Bentley's Miscellany*, and from then on all his major novels were published as serial instalments in his own magazines.

In 1842, now an internationally famous author, Dickens travelled to America, to visit for himself this new haven of democracy and undertake a lecture tour. He was disappointed by what he found there, and most prominent was his condemnation of slavery which he attacked in the account of his travels, *American Notes*. Dickens took breaks from novel writing living abroad in Italy, in 1844, and in Switzerland, in 1846. He also returned to America in 1867 in order to extend his reading tours to the New World.

After over twenty years of marriage, in 1858, Dickens abruptly separated from his wife Catherine, mother of his ten children, in order to pursue a relationship with Ellen Ternan, a young actress. He died suddenly in 1870, leaving his novel, *The Mystery of Edwin Drood*, unfinished.

Pete Orford gained his PhD from the Shakespeare Institute for researching the modern reception of Shakespeare's history plays. Since then he has become embroiled in an academic ménage à trois with Shakespeare and Dickens, presenting papers at conferences on both writers, as well as publishing articles and books. He is the general editor of *Divining Thoughts: Future Directions in Shakespeare Studies* and is currently working on forthcoming collections of Dickens' writings for Hesperus Press, including *On London* and *On Theatre*.